"Spec"
williana
Nixon
Vickers
5AC cow
Fred

MW00585663

In the
BIG THICKET
On the Trail of the
WILD MAN

EXPLORING NATURE'S MYSTERIOUS DIMENSION

ROB RIGGS

uncle fount simmons
ggg uncle

PARAVIEW PRESS

NEW YORK

In the Big Thicket, On the Trail of the Wild Man
Copyright © 2001 by Rob Riggs
All rights reserved. No part of this book may be used or reproduced in
any manner whatsoever without prior written permission, except for the
inclusion of brief quotations in reviews. For more information contact
Paraview Press, 1674 Broadway, Suite 4B, New York, NY 10019, or visit
our website at www.paraviewpress.com.

Grateful acknowledgment is made to the following for their kind
permission to reprint copyright material: Buddy Moore, "It Seemed Like a
Huge Hairy Ape-like Creature, said a Fink," *Kountze News,* July 19, 1979.
The Beaumont Enterprise for the article "Strange blackout draws different
theories," by Kevin Carmody, May 3, 1985.

Cover photograph by Reneé Leger Schwab
Back cover photographs by Rob Riggs and Bill Fleming
Book design by smythtype
Map design by Reneé Judkins

ISBN: 1-931044-26-0

Library of Congress Catalog Card Number: 2001089104

THIS WORK IS DEDICATED *to Bonnie Poss Riggs, Liston Riggs, Homer Riggs, Ethel Parker Poss, Brazos Riggs, and to all my friends and relations who inspired me with their lives and now rest in the arms of God; and to my sons, Jacob and Jordan, that they may not forget their rich heritage.*

Contents

CHAPTER 1   **The Lair of the Mysterious** / 7

CHAPTER 2   **The Ghost Light** / 21

CHAPTER 3   **The Wild Man** / 66

CHAPTER 4   **The Indian Mysteries** / 107

CHAPTER 5   **The Hole in the Earth** / 135

CHAPTER 6   **Seeing Things Differently** / 168

Acknowledgments / 179

Bibliography / 182

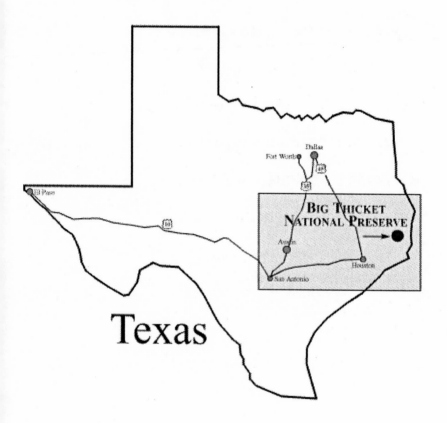

Texas

CHAPTER 1

The Lair
of the Mysterious

Bill thought we'd better take along some serious self-defense. The stories I had been telling him about the "wild man" sightings in the Big Thicket finally piqued his curiosity enough for him to join me on an exploratory hike. He drove in from the Central Texas Hill Country to rural Hardin County in deep Southeast Texas and brought an M-14 semi-automatic assault rifle and a .38 special police revolver with him.

We entered the Big Thicket National Preserve at the Little Pine Island Bayou Corridor Unit with the intention of following the bayou upstream to the Kountze-Sour Lake Highway. This would cover a distance of some 10 to 12 miles through swampy woods, vine-entangled palmetto flats and heavy underbrush. There had been a number of wild man sightings in that general area over a considerable length of time, enough to suggest that the drainage area of the bayou might be part of its territory or range.

Bill brought the guns and I didn't object. The Constable in Sour Lake had already questioned my sanity a number of times for going into the woods alone, especially alone and unarmed–not so much for my lack of protection from snakes and razorback hogs and the like as from some of the two-legged denizens of those woods who are legendary for their bad attitudes.

The Big Thicket was famous as a refuge for outlaws and reprobates for over a hundred years. There are still plenty of citizens of its deeper reaches who believe that hunting laws are

Communist-inspired and that game wardens make excellent trot-line bait. The "Dog People," as they are called for their custom of illegally poaching deer by running them down with packs of hounds, are never far from their shotguns. They are also highly suspicious, and are prone to assume that any stranger they might encounter in their woods is likely to be some kind of Yankee federal agent up to no good.

The Constable recommended two essential pieces of equipment if I was fool enough to disregard his advice—a good pistol of at least 9mm caliber that would take down an adversary even if only nicked in the shoulder, and a pair of "Big Thicket house shoes." He noticed approvingly that I already had a pair of knee-high rubber boots, and he just happened to have an extra 9mm pistol that he would sell me, even if somewhat illicitly at the time, for a good price.

What the Constable didn't suspect was that I had considerable reason to believe that there is more than one two-legged species native to the Thicket. What I didn't even attempt to explain to him was that I felt somehow that this other species would sense it if I were armed and is intelligent enough to keep itself hidden even if it were keenly and stealthily observing me. I had good intentions toward the wild man and, naively perhaps, had faith that it would understand that. As foolish as it might seem, I was willing to give it the jump on me just for the chance of seeing it and satisfying my curiosity. I did wonder, though, if I could outrun that old Booger, particularly with those damn rubber boots on.

Thus, I decided not to buy a gun for myself. I was frankly glad to have a willing companion in Bill for this particular trip, though, and after advising him of the risks involved, acceded to his judgment that we should not go unarmed. About a half hour into the woods we paused for awhile and practiced firing the guns. The rifle had a strong kick and was so loud it left our ears ringing.

We shot at pine cones and dead branches of trees that had long ago jammed the slow-moving currents of the tea-colored water. All the while I wondered what kind of protection these guns would afford us if we were to actually encounter the elusive man/creature. If the sightings stories were as reputable as they seemed, it could be something formidable to deal with. And it wasn't just a matter of whether our arms were of sufficient caliber to bring it down, should we have a hostile encounter.

There was something strange about the sightings stories, something that suggested that the creature has an intelligence, maybe even a psychic nature, that gives an other-worldly quality to it, as if it were a nightmare somehow materialized into the real world. But it was this weird aspect of the stories and of my own experience that I found so compelling.

We trudged through some of the thickest woods in North America, staying as close to the bayou as possible. In the vast green sea of trees, whose dense canopy prevented us from even using the sun for guidance, the bayou provided the only landmark to avoid getting lost without having to constantly refer to a compass. The woods were also more open and the going easier in the flood plain.

The passing hours slowly accumulated into the better part of a day without anything happening of much consequence. But the water in several stretches of the bayou was remarkable; where it was normally muddy or clear-brown, today it was clear and blue. Then we came to a tributary near the confluence of Black Creek, where swamp water as black as crude oil protrudes into one of the blue holes. This meant we were nearing the end of our hike, and that we were no more than an hour or so from the highway. Then we heard it.

Bill noticed it first. From my days of birding and many hours spent in the woods I recognized it as the cry of a hawk. There was something peculiar about it, though. As we stood silent and listened, we realized that these were distress calls. Something was causing that hawk considerable grief. Then its cries were abruptly cut off.

It's hard to judge the direction and distance of sound in the deep woods, but we began to suspect that the hawk had been just upstream from where we were when we first heard it. It occurred to us that the hawk had been shot or otherwise had met some dreadful end, but we had not heard any gun shots or any sounds other than the hawk's distressed cries. Even if the hawk had met its demise, the odds of our actually finding it were very remote in woods that thick. That's what made it so remarkable that we soon did find the hawk—or what was left of it.

It was directly in our path where a dim game trail, traced probably by deer and feral hogs, crossed a small clearing by the bayou. At the base of a huge pine tree we found the wings, tail feathers, legs, and talons of an extremely unlucky Cooper's Hawk. There is little question it was the same hawk. The talons were still limp, and the tendons, ragged and exposed where the legs had been ripped from the hawk's body, were still moist.

It was as if something had taken this poor bird by the feet, spread its legs, chomped down on it, and swallowed it whole after spitting out the less digestible parts. You may know something that can do this to a hawk, but I don't.

There were no obvious clues in the clearing, no tracks or signs of a struggle. I could think of no natural predators that would even be inclined to attack a fairly good sized hawk, which is itself a predator. There are only a few animals native to the Thicket that would even be large enough, and most of these such as coyotes, foxes, bobcats, cougars, or maybe a Great Horned owl are nocturnal and wouldn't be likely to hunt in broad daylight. We had neither seen nor heard any signs of dogs during the entire hike.

It would be very unlikely that any of these animals could catch a hawk on the ground. Even if the hawk had been wounded and was disabled and already on the ground, it is unlikely that any of these animals could do what was done to this poor bird without leaving any tracks in the muddy clearing.

You may think that there is an entirely reasonable explanation for this event and that it was merely coincidental that we just happened to be there, no matter how unusual it was. Bill and I were equally sure, with the kind of uncanny feeling you get when you're in an unfamiliar place and sense that you are being watched by unseen and sinister eyes, that someone or something intended for us to understand that it could tear us apart limb from limb just as easily as it had that unfortunate hawk.

I couldn't help but wonder if whoever or whatever had done this would have revealed itself if we hadn't implied hostile intent by having the guns with us. Bill, ever more vigilant than me, wondered what that someone or something would have done to us if we hadn't had the guns. We got the message. We were on unfamiliar ground. We had blundered, even if intentionally, into someone else's territory, and we were lucky. Like a good-natured policeman will sometimes do with a first time traffic offender—this time we were just given a warning.

The preface of an obscure medieval spiritual text cautions its potential readership: "If you still cherish your tender, delicate flesh, do not read the rest of this book." This admonition is only a little too strong for the book you now hold in your hands. If your primary concerns in life are comfort and security and you have no taste for adventure and discovery, if your personal reality map is set just the way you want it, then stand forewarned. If you continue reading, you may enter unfamiliar territory that could be just a little bit uncomfortable.

This book discusses things that are not supposed to exist, and events that are not supposed to happen, at least according to conventional wisdom of polite society. You will be challenged to think what you might have thought unthinkable, and you will find evidence that the unknown sometimes makes profound intrusions into what we comfortably take to be the natural order of things.

You will read about the half ape/half human "wild men" that wander the deep woods at night, and occasionally even the town margins and suburbs, howling like banshees; about black "panthers" with self-luminous eyes whose high-pitched screams sound like those of terrified women; and about "ghost lights" that knock out the engines of automobiles, exhibit signs of curiosity and intelligence, and chase carloads of terrified, though willing, observers at high speeds down a famous country dirt road.

There will be accounts of events like unidentified lights seen in the night skies above Southeast Texas and Southwest Louisiana as the electrical utility for virtually the entire region is mysteriously blacked-out; and independent sightings by different witnesses who were attacked in the deep swamp by primitive Indians who were supposed to have vanished more than a century ago.

In the Big Thicket region such events and sightings are not mere isolated instances embellished by over-active imaginations. There have been numerous reports of this kind in the same general area for decades—enough reports to show patterns and to suggest that these various phenomena may be related and ultimately have a common source.

In case you're thinking that the only relation these phenomena could possibly have would be of the type believable only by regular readers of the supermarket tabloids, please stand assured that there is not one account herein of an Elvis sighting in the Big Thicket. These tales are not mere tabloid-style fabrications, as the phenomena that occur there are legitimized by the fact that they appear to be part of a global pattern of similar, if not identical, phenomena to which the Big Thicket phenomena in turn lend credibility. The published works of American researchers Loren Coleman and John Keel and British researchers Paul Devereux, David Clarke and Janet and Colin Bord, among others, document the widespread occurrence of such sightings.

What I hope to demonstrate in this book is the considerable evidence that all of these phenomena are related to witnesses' responses to localized and periodic fluctuations of a peculiar type of energy. While the intensity and focusing of this energy may be related to the earth's magnetic field, and perhaps to sunspot activity, its exact source and nature and the reasons for its recurrent fluctuations in wild places like the Big Thicket remain essentially unknown.

The peculiar energy involved in the various sightings events presented in this material apparently has disturbing, even bizarre, effects on the human mind. This is not to suggest, however, that the strange creatures and events witnessed in the Thicket are mere hallucinations or instances of mass hysteria. Hallucinations don't leave footprints or claw marks or burn the paint on cars. When the energy in these fields is active in places like the Big Thicket, it seems almost as if the very fabric of what we call reality becomes temporarily unraveled.

Though my research and conclusions will draw on the work of others, this book is based for the most part on my own personal experiences and on interviews with eyewitnesses. To an extent it is also based on third person accounts, but only when they contain salient elements that, unknown to the witnesses, corroborate stories taken from different sightings. Otherwise, stories not coming from reputable eyewitnesses I have dismissed as unreliable hearsay. In every case, I have given preference to sightings with multiple witnesses, which tend to be more reliable.

I have made very attempt to avoid references to what might be merely apocryphal stories or folklore that does not relate to specifically documentable incidences. When I do cite folklore as an example of how these phenomena affect local culture in the areas where they occur, I identify it as such.

The events and sightings on which this book is based all took place within the same general area. This demonstrates that the entire range of unusual phenomena cited from the body of research, including recurrent standing ghost light locations, widespread power outages, UFO sightings, large hairy "wild man" and mystery black cat sightings have all been known to recur for generations, with considerable regularity of an as yet undetermined periodicity, within a localized area in the Big Thicket region of Southeast Texas. Much of the area is contained within a federally protected biological preserve that was set aside in large part for scientific research. That being the case, this book should be considered in large part as a call for research in what might be Nature's ideal natural laboratory for field research of such phenomena.

My emphasis will be less on documenting and detailing individual episodes. This has already been done admirably and thoroughly by others. What I will emphasize here is how the pattern of events as evidenced in the Big Thicket lends support to the suggestion, made by other researchers, that there is a chain of causality and interrelation that points to a common source for the various phenomena.

We live in an increasingly urban, technological and synthetic environment that leaves most of us cut off from any substantial or prolonged contact with Nature, either physically or psychologically. Could there be evidence of a natural force involved in perception that has gone ignored? Would this particularly be the case if it were involved with what might be called a psychic environment, which has itself been virtually forgotten? What would happen if one were to find oneself in an unfamiliar environment, such as the deep woods, and suddenly thrust into a face-to-face encounter with something totally outside the range of ordinary experience? The answers to such questions might surprise you.

The body of research presented here suggests that there are fundamentals of the mechanics of the way we see the world, if not the way the world itself is constructed, that are not fully understood and maybe even little suspected. It suggests that there are factors in our environment, such as ambient electromagnetic fields, that affect and inform the act of perception in subtle ways that also have yet to be fully understood.

If this seems a little too abstract, you should know that the strange goings-on in the Big Thicket, particularly those relating to the mysterious Bragg Light, have been sufficiently persistent and contain enough objective reality to have attracted the attention of hard science since the 1950s. At first this consisted mainly of attempts to debunk the stories by attempting to explain them away as naive, if not hysterical, misperceptions of entirely ordinary natural phenomena. Increasingly, though, even scientists have come to acknowledge that, indeed, something extraordinary is happening in the Big Thicket and in other wild places documented by legitimate researchers all over America and the world.

The work of such eminent and internationally respected scientists as Yoshi-Hiko Ohtsuki of Japan and neuroscientist Michael Persinger of Canada lends legitimacy to the reality of the occurrences and the unknown nature of the kinds of unusual phenomena that recur in the Big Thicket. My emphasis here, however, will not be to explain away the sightings in scientific terms, nor even to attempt to prove that the things people see in the Big Thicket woods actually exist in the way that we normally think of how things exist.

What I hope to demonstrate is that the weird phenomena encountered in wild places cannot be totally accounted for within the tenets of the unquestioned and naively materialistic empiricism that so dominates modern science. This kind of science summarily dismisses experiences of the mysterious dimension of life and relegates them to what is called the paranormal. It may well be that there is more to Nature than the exclusively quantitative and analytical methods of science can appreciate, and that with a greater appreciation of this mysterious dimension, the definition of what is normal and natural may have to be expanded.

Even after all these considerations, you may be asking yourself why anyone would want to know about these things. What does it matter that strange lights, ape-like wild men, and other weird things are sometimes seen in wild places, except to know to avoid them? You may have the attitude of my old friend Larry Baker from Sour Lake.

Larry grew up hearing many of the same stories I did, and he used to run a paper route that took him on remote roads in the Big Thicket in the wee hours of the morning. He had seen both panthers and bears during his rounds, which at the time were not officially supposed to still exist in the area, so it wasn't hard for me to convince him that there were wild men in the Thicket. But his attitude was that he believed those wild men were doing fine just where they are, and he saw no reason to mess with them.

If this is your attitude, and you are comfortable with your understanding of yourself and the world, or if you acknowledge that there are mysteries in the world but think that there are some that are better left alone, you are certainly not to be blamed. There is much to be learned, though, both about ourselves and the nature of the world, for those who are willing to take the risks. There are risks involved with entering into the Unknown, (remember what happened to the poor hawk), but risk is the price of discovery. This book is for those of us who seem to have no choice but to take the risks.

Many of you may even have had the kinds of encounters and seen the types of creatures and lights that are described in this work. In fact, the odds are that even if you haven't had such an experience, someone you know has and has told you about it. You may have received little encouragement to talk about or try to understand your experience. This book will hopefully provide some encouragement. It is for those of us who sense from our own encounters with the mysterious dimension of our lives that "something is going on" despite denials from academic, scientific, governmental and other supposedly authoritative sources.

What we need is an approach to research in this area that gives in to neither the inherent cynicism of unquestioned scientism nor to the true believer fervor of trekkie UFO buffs. What is called for and what must be consistently applied is an open-minded appeal to reason and to actual human experience that does not deny that strange things may sometimes be witnessed just because they do not fit into some "expert's" preconceived definition of what is possible.

Given the weird things that sometimes happen in wild places, we might just need to take a philosophical attitude and learn to look at things in a little different way. These are more than isolated bizarre instances. They are reminders, welling up from our deepest unconscious selves, that mystery is the essence of what we are and we are inherently connected to that which is beyond the limitations of our finite and temporal existence.

You may wonder what qualifies an old newspaperman to philosophize and elaborate on such subtleties. Nobody with his eyes and ears open could have been in the newspaper business for as long as I have without noticing that the world simply does not work in the way that the culture at large assures us it is supposed to work. This is especially noticeable if you've ever worked at a paper in or near a wild place like the Big Thicket.

There's something almost palpable about such a place that works its way into the mass psyche, and even people who may not have actually had a vivid encounter or strange experience may also be affected in subtle ways. Part of this effect, I'm convinced, comes from what can only be called the awe or fear with which the weird aspects of such places are regarded by those of us who are stuck in our comfortable but habitual and routine lives. The Big Thicket is simply a spooky place, and it is a common experience, even among experienced campers and outdoors enthusiasts, that a night in the woods there will put the fear in you. As my dear friend, the late Jerry Mount of Pine Ridge, used to say, "there are places in those woods where Moses wouldn't go." It is dark and foreboding to even the most casual observer. It participates in all the mystique of the great southern cypress swamps, of which it is the western extent. Like all swamplands it is a keen mirror of that shadowy part of the human mind in which we hide our deepest fears. Even those who are most familiar with it and who live in and around it are not immune to the creepy feelings the Thicket can inspire. For many this kind of fear has a spiritual dimension, and like Lincoln said, "The fear of the Lord is the beginning of wisdom."

My first boss in the newspaper business, Buddy Moore, used to run a column in the *Kountze News,* his paper at the time, that was written by a shade tree mechanic by the name of John Wacasey. It wasn't a column on automotive repair, however. It was about the author's views on religion and philosophy, complete with all of his misspellings and grammatical atrocities. Our readers used to call us almost daily to complain about this fellow's column. I asked Buddy how he could continue to run such a poorly written feature that sometimes ran up to a half page. Buddy would just grin and assure me that all the people that were complaining about the column couldn't wait until the paper came out every week just so they could read it and complain about it.

"Let me tell you something I've learned from experience that has served me well in this business," Buddy said. "There are more theologians and philosophers per square mile in Hardin County, Texas, than anywhere in the world."

At the time I didn't really appreciate what Buddy meant, but I suspect now that he wasn't talking about uneducated backwoods people merely arguing their prejudices. Something about the rural Big Thicket environment may have contributed to an ambient atmosphere conducive to a genuine inquiry. Their inquiries may not have been particularly rational according to so-called educated standards, but they were nonetheless sincere and perhaps inspired.

The Thicket entices those who venture into its depths, and maybe even some of those who just live along its edges, to naturally ponder the mysteries of life—not as some intellectual abstraction, not even from an appreciation of the luxuriant botanical diversity for which this East Texas jungle is justifiably famous, but from direct experience of something both indefinable and tangible about its brooding presence.

The late Archer Fullingim, Buddy's predecessor at the *Kountze News* and a nationally acclaimed and widely respected Texas newspaperman, was apparently conscious of this influence, and it had spiritual significance for him as well. He called that part of the woods within the Hardin County triangle formed by Kountze, Saratoga and Sour Lake, the "Holy Ghost Thicket" from a feeling he sometimes got on his outings there.

He described his transcendent experience thus, "I sat down against a tree. and I sat there and pretty soon this feeling washed over me like a wind in my heart and I felt like I'd been there before. I was suffused with a spirit something like what Adam and Eve must have felt. It's a feeling of lightness."

Don Moser quoted Fullingim further on this point in an interview that was part of an article for *National Geographic* magazine. What did Archer mean by the Holy Ghost Thicket? "Now listen at me," he replied, "I can tell I'm in the Big Thicket by the feelin' I get. It's a kind of religion to me. Down there along Black Creek, I call it the Holy Ghost Thicket—you get a mysterious, supernatural feelin'. You look at those yellow and green toadstools, and the overstory of trees, and hear the birds sing. This is where I get the charge, the feeling, the—-the kicks."

Archer's revelation testifies to an important aspect of encounters with the strange energies in the Thicket, and to why it might serve us well to understand them. Not everyone has a frightening experience of monstrous forms and ghoulish lights. Sometimes the encounters may be uplifting and revelatory. Either type of experience attests to that mostly forgotten and neglected dimension of our essential mysterious nature without which we are maybe not fully human.

Something of this same effect has been expressed eloquently by East Texas folklorist Francis Abernethy. Of the Thicket he writes, "It represents the Great Unknown to the mind cluttered with trade names in a society labeled and categorized." And further, "It is the individual's final fortress against civilization. To those who talk about it, the Big Thicket stands for something else, too; it is the lair of the mysterious."

So come along, if you dare, for a stomp in the swamp and a trek in the forest primeval. If you keep your courage up, your eyes open, and your wits about you, you just might come out of these enchanted old woods seeing things a little bit differently. It might ~n make a philosopher out of you, too.

CHAPTER 2

The Ghost Light

"That damned light was alive!" Jim's voice expressed both conviction and astonishment, and the look on his face told me he was more than just trying to convince me. He was also struggling to admit to himself what he had seen that night on Bragg Road. His experience haunted him with something he didn't want to think about, much less talk about, and something he was sure no one else would believe. For over thirty years he kept it to himself, fearful of censure and perhaps afraid for his own sanity, and he never even told his wife, Mary, about what he saw.

She was a student of mine in English class in Beaumont at the time Jim brought his story to me, and she had told him about my research. Mary knew that Jim (last names withheld by request) had an interest in the ghost light on Bragg Road, but she never suspected the depth of his interest or the trauma that the place held for him. There was, then, a certain element of relief for him in approaching me with this information. Here, at last, was someone who might listen to his story without doubting his sanity, and who maybe could help him deal with a genuine encounter with the Unknown that his conscious mind and beliefs had forced him to repress for so long.

What makes Jim's reluctance to talk about his encounter on the infamous "Ghost Road" and the experience itself all the more remarkable is that his experience did not occur in a social atmosphere of ridicule and disbelief. Indeed, prior to Jim's sighting literally thousands of Southeast Texans for generations had already traveled in small groups of one or two couples or carloads of curious would-be witnesses to actually seek out the very object that so traumatized Jim—the legendary "Ghost Light."

Making trips to the Ghost Road had long been a tradition in the area and was widely considered a harmless activity for teenagers and a wholesome outing for the entire family. Untold numbers of those who had had this adventure over the decades claimed to have actually seen the light. Jim probably knew some of those who had seen or thought they had seen it, and maybe even some who had bragged about it. Usually such sightings, though, occurred at a distance of a few hundred yards up to a mile or more of the road's arrow-straight eight-mile length. These could only have been sightings of car lights filtered through the tunnel effect created by trees on each side of the road whose canopies enmesh over the roadbed. Yes, they could have seen something else, but there was always this rational explanation from skeptics. Jim's encounter was a little more up close and personal.

More than a few of those who claim to have seen the light have been back dozens of times for the fun of it. Jim didn't think what he experienced was any fun at all. In fact, he has never been back to Bragg Road since that fateful night when something for which he had no wrinkle in his brain rather rudely rearranged his belief structures. In many respects, though, the story of Jim's sighting started out no differently from those of thousands of other Southeast Texans, and to recall his story is to typify the stories of many others.

Like most kids from the area, Jim had heard the ghost light stories for about as long as he could remember. The fame of the mysterious light, said to appear on Bragg Road just north of Saratoga, had long been established in the small towns and rural communities around Beaumont and near the Louisiana border. Going to search for the light was almost a rite of passage for teenagers in the area, so it was almost inevitable that Jim would eventually make his personal pilgrimage to the Ghost Road.

One Saturday night, when faced with the uninteresting prospect of spending the evening cruising 11th street in Beaumont or maybe hanging out in a shopping center parking lot, Jim and two buddies decided instead to make their first trip in search of the light. The drive out into the backwoods of Hardin County gave the boys about a half hour to savor what they hoped would be their initiation into the mysteries of the light, or what would at least be a mild adventure.

As they made their way out Hwy. 105 into the heart of the Big Thicket country, the boys goaded one another with what they knew about the legends of the ghost light. One story claimed the light was the lantern of a phantom railroad brake man who is still looking for his head lost in an accident when Bragg Road was still the right-of-way for an old railroad. Another said the light is the torch of a night hunter still trying to find his way out of the Thicket after being lost for ages in the dense, swampy woods. These stories are part of the established folklore of the region and were well known to the boys.

Like most healthy skeptics the boys thought these were no more than tall tales, quaint reminders of a simpler time when science had not yet explained away the mystery from such things. No doubt the boys thought there was a reasonable explanation for the light. Probably it was distant car lights, which is what most people really believed. Maybe it was swamp gas. Some scientists had done a brief study and concluded that. But these down-to-earth considerations did not entirely detract from their sense of anticipation.

The Ghost Road is surrounded by gloomy, impenetrable woods where even the bravest and most cynical are reluctant to venture at night. A spookier place is hard to imagine. A spur-of-the-moment midnight trip there was at least good for a few macho points. If they saw anything remotely mysterious, they could claim that they saw the Light. That's what they imagined was the source of the stories anyway, and there was no harm in joining in the fun. At the very least they could scope out a good place to park, and that was the real reason they figured Bragg Road was so popular with teen-agers.

The boys arrived at about midnight and drove directly up about five miles of the Ghost Road's straight-shot eight-mile length. They stopped the car, turned off its lights and left the engine running. Just as they were trying to decide whether to sit and wait or turn back, they were greeted by an eerie, diffuse-orange glow.

It issued from the pitch-black woods to their right. Jim described it as being "like what would precede a lantern entering a dark room." The glow emitted from a six-inch ball of brilliant orangeish light that came to hover less than twenty feet in front of them. Their astonishment turned to terror as the light approached with movements that seemed conscious and deliberate. It stopped just to the right of the car that was still idling. Slowly, it moved across the hood, causing the engine to stall. Frantically, the boys were able to restart the engine as the light came to rest to the left of their car. They took off down Bragg Road just as fast as its unpaved sandy surface would allow. The light pursued them and easily kept pace with the car at speeds approaching fifty miles per hour. After about two miles, and without slowing down, the light made an abrupt ninety degree turn to the left, ascended above the treetops, and disappeared in a streak of unimaginable speed. The entire episode lasted for over five minutes.

This chase scene alone would be enough to leave anyone with a lifetime of recurring nightmares. This is not how swamp gas or car beam reflections, or anything else that we know about for that matter, is known to act. The sudden shock of a direct confrontation with something so totally outside the range of normal experience made Jim's reaction somewhat understandable, but what really traumatized him into a thirty-year silence, and what he could not bring himself to admit, was the behavior of the light and how it seemed to react to him and his friends.

As it moved across the hood of their car like a huge, glowing, disembodied eyeball, the terror of Jim and his friends convinced them that it was watching them intently, like a wild animal would that was both curious and coldly anticipating the next move of its intended prey. The light acted like it knew what it was doing, as if it were a conscious, intelligent being.

You might have trouble believing Jim's story. He even had trouble believing it himself. If his were an isolated case, we might doubt the details of his account, question his integrity or sanity, or at least seek a simple explanation. Jim's story, however, is only slightly more spectacular than a multitude of others with which it shares specific details. Any one of these tales, taken separately, might be easily dismissed, but taken together they weave a complex, intricate fabric of tales, legends, and sightings accounts with enough common elements to give them at least some credibility. The tales of braggarts, out-and-out liars and well-intended wishful thinkers who may only think they have seen the light undoubtedly make up the vast majority of ghost light accounts related to Bragg Road. As long-time Hardin County newspaper publisher, Buddy Moore, once told me, "If you just think you saw the Light, you ain't seen it." There are plenty of stories from people like Jim who don't just think they saw the real deal on the Ghost Road. To them it is useless to trot out theories of car lights and swamp gas.

One such story came to me from an old friend who was a school teacher and coach at Sour Lake during my days of attendance there. Henry Pitts was from an old Hardin County family, who as he said, grew up running barefoot up and down Village Creek killing water moccasins with a stick. With this background he was an accomplished woodsman and was also very knowledgeable of the lore of the Big Thicket woods.

Prior to starting a career in education he had served as a highway patrolman for the state. At one time Bragg Road had been in his territory and he frequently patrolled it at night. On several occasions the light chased him at high speeds. Here was a man who knew whereof he spoke. He knew what swamp gas looks like and assured me that the ghost light was definitely not swamp gas.

Another source of this type of story are the writings of Francis Abernethy, a professor at Stephen F. Austin University in Nacogdoches and a noted East Texas folklorist. He traces stories of "The Saratoga Light" to around the turn of the century. Beginning in about 1960 the fame of the light began to grow and attract hundreds of would-be viewers. Abernethy reports that during that period, Archer Fullingim, publisher of the *Kountze News,* invited scientists to study the phenomenon. They concluded generally and somewhat vaguely that the light was gaseous.

Others thought the light was no more than the reflection of headlight beams from cars on the Saratoga-to-Votaw highway as they made a curve near where Bragg Road intersects with the highway. Many Thicketeers were unconvinced by these arguments and insisted that the ghost light is of a more mysterious nature. In particular were those of whose accounts Abernethy wrote, "According to reports that came out of the Thicket during this period, the Light went wild. It chased cars; it floated over the hoods and cut out engines; it burned hands and scorched car tops." As we will see, stories of this type did not end in the 1960s.

Some might object that people are inclined to see what they already believe in and that such gullibility is the source of the sightings. Jim would argue with this. He had the opposite problem of having a hard time believing what he was seeing. There have also been cases of former staunch unbelievers and skeptics who have been converted by dramatic and inexplicable encounters with the ghost light.

Roxanne Kuebodeaux and her family frequently traveled on Bragg Road at night during the hunting season to get to their deer lease in the adjacent woods. For years they saw nothing mysterious and skeptically dismissed the legends. Their skepticism was abruptly shattered one night when they were confronted by a light that appeared suddenly and directly in their path. Startled, they swerved and stopped their pickup, thinking the light was an oncoming vehicle. No sooner had they stopped than the light moved to hover above the hood. Not only did it stall their engine, as in Jim's case, it also burned the paint on the pickup's hood.

Mr. Boudreaux, a native and life-long resident of Saratoga, flatly did not believe in the ghost light. He had been to Bragg Road many times during the years, including the traditional teenage outings. His opinion was that if there were any lights on Bragg Road other than car lights, they were Bud Lights, the effects of which, in his mind, accounted for all the stories. Boudreaux's opinion was changed, however, during an illegal but altogether too typical Hardin County night hunt for wild razorback hogs.

His hunting party had just bagged two of the pineywoods rooters just off the ghost road and were busy trying to load their prey into their pickup. Suddenly, a light appeared in the near distance. At first the men were only mildly alarmed, thinking it was just an approaching car whose occupants, in the frontier ethic of the Thicket, could damn well mind their own business. As the light came closer it became obvious that it was not a car. There was only one light that loomed larger and larger. The men began to panic as it occurred to them that they had been caught red-handed by a game warden with one hell of a big flashlight.

Not until the light had come right upon them did they realize that it was, indeed, the infamous ghost light. Try to imagine the mind-set of someone who is shocked into the sudden realization that, not only is something that he has always dismissed as a fantasy actually real, but that it is also unimaginably weird. Boudreaux described his and his companions' response in his inimitable accent: "You ain't ever seen two hawgs git throwed in the back of a truck so fast!"

Perhaps even more interesting than cases of such sudden converts are those coming from people who once thought they had seen the light but who later had more vivid and convincing experiences. I heard the following story during an appearance on a radio talk show in Beaumont. The host was not altogether convinced by the accounts I was giving him and was actually spending more time airing his doubts than he was letting me speak, when we received a call from a gentleman with the following, very compelling story.

A gentleman who identified himself only as Lee from Trout Creek in an adjoining county estimates that he had made the trip to Bragg Road some thirty times over the years. On several occasions he had seen something in the distance he assumed, or maybe hoped, was the ghost light. Many of his friends were unconvinced by his accounts, so one night he decided to take a camera with him to record whatever he might see. He and his wife had not been on Bragg Road for long when a dazzling bluish-white sphere about the size of a basketball suddenly "blinked on" not far from them at treetop level.

They watched in amazement as the light acrobatically bobbed and wove, dancing to and fro across the road bed, all the while maintaining its distance from its stunned observers. After about a minute the light rose slightly above the trees and streaked away to their left. Lee was so astonished by the light's sudden appearance and mesmeric behavior that he completely forgot about his camera. He failed to get the proof he had hoped to show his doubting friends. Any lingering doubts he may have had about the reality of the light's existence, however, were thoroughly dispelled. No longer did he just think he had seen the light—he knew it; and he also knew—in a way he did not expect anyone to believe or understand—that the light had also seen him.

Despite hearing and collecting such graphic accounts as these, it wasn't until I saw the light for myself that I was entirely convinced that it really exists as a genuine unknown. After numerous trips to Bragg Road and some twenty years after my first trip, I talked a friend from Austin into making the trip with me. Stan must have brought me luck, for within an hour of our arrival, the light showed up.

It appeared suddenly about thirty feet in front of our slowly moving vehicle. We were headed north, away from the direction of the Votaw-bound traffic and with the suspect car light beams to our backs. It was as if a light bulb had been turned on. The light was sharply defined, spherical, and about the size of a basketball. It glowed with a bluish-white luminosity, drifted slowly to our right for a span of a few seconds, and blinked off.

Such stories have not convinced everyone of the reality of the Bragg Light or of its mysterious nature. The topic is always the subject of lively debate even in Hardin County where the light has been seen for so many years by so many different people. It might surprise you, then, to know that for generations literally hundreds of locations world-wide have reported the same general description and behavior of ghost lights as the Big Thicket ghost light. In many cases, there have been more than enough documented sightings for a long enough period to have developed a folklore similar to the Bragg Light and to have generated the same kinds of controversies as occur in Southeast Texas.

More than thirty such places exist in the United States alone. One of the best-known occurs in the mountains of the Trans-Pecos region of far West Texas, between the small towns of Alpine and Marfa, where the Marfa Lights have been seen by about as many generations of West Texans as the Bragg Light has been seen by East Texans.

Other well-known ghost lights include the Brown Mountain Light of North Carolina, the Hornet Spook Light of Missouri, the Pinnacles Light of California, the Yakima Indian Reservation light in Washington, and the light that appears near Gonzales, Louisiana. Paul Devereux and David Clarke of Great Britain have written extensively of traditional ghost light locations in the British Isles and other parts of Europe and in Asia and Australia.

Whether they are called ghost lights, spook lights, earth lights, or unusual luminous or light-form phenomena, a growing international body of scholars and scientists has come to accept these lights as part of a global phenomenon worthy of serious study. Usually the lights are about the size and shape of a basketball and may vary from bluish to reddish white. Appearances may occur within a range of a few miles, but they are all localized around a general central area.

There is no reliable information about the frequency of the lights' appearances. On any given night one might go to a ghost light location and see nothing, but over an extended period the chances for a legitimate observation would certainly increase.

The unanimous opinion of ghost light researchers is that the lights represent some little understood manifestation of the earth's electromagnetic energy field. This conclusion is based on repeated reports of electrical disturbances associated with the lights. The stopping of car engines and blackouts of car lighting systems and radios that we have already seen associated with the light on Bragg Road, while not occurring in all encounters with the lights, are not uncommon. Such research, however, does not scientifically explain away the mystery of the ghost lights, nor does it even present a consistent theory that accounts for their existence. Instead, as will become increasingly evident in this narrative, the ghost lights, in terms of their origin, nature, and especially their behavior, do not neatly conform to a simple electromagnetic theory. That's why the ghost light locations and the various phenomena that occur in them are so important for us to understand.

Paranormal phenomena are often justifiably criticized as being too subjective. If a person claims to have seen a UFO or unusual light-form, to have had an alien visitor or abduction experience, or to have seen a Bigfoot or unusual humanoid creature, too often we are left only with his or her word for it and have no assurance that the person was not just imagining things. Usually there is no evidence that there is any objective reality of any kind involved. The witness cannot duplicate the experience or reproduce the conditions leading to it in a way that is discernible to anyone else. In other words the experiences are subjective and real only to the person involved.

In the case of the ghost lights, however, there is an objective element with physical manifestations. In them we have what might be called unexplained phenomena exhibiting paranormal characteristics with tangible parameters. When Jim and Roxanne and their friends saw the light on Bragg Road, they were seeing something outside normal experience and perception, indeed, something apparently outside our understanding of the way the Universe is supposed to work. There was, however, no question that their sightings existed only in their imaginations. Imaginations do not cause car engines to stall or disrupt their electrical systems. They definitely saw something that had enough objective physical reality to cause these effects, and as we shall see, what they saw was much more than just unusual.

I hope to demonstrate in the pages to follow that in the locations and phenomena of the ghost light areas we may have a unique opportunity to observe the link between the subjective and the objective, between mind and matter, and between the imagination and reality. These are not claims idly made, nor are they made ill-advisedly, ignoring scientific facts. Indeed, before we can realize how profoundly significant these phenomena are we must first consider what science has to say about them. There is no need to merely make romantic assertions, nor should this inquiry be accused of intellectual dishonesty. If genuinely weird things really do happen in ghost light areas, a logical, scientific investigation should confirm the presence of that very quality of weirdness.

My associate, Bill Fleming, makes a point in this regard that is appropriate here. Bill is affectionately known among a small circle of his friends as the "Medicine Man" from his broad knowledge of the shamanic practices of his American Indian heritage. He uses the word "medicine" the way the Indians once did. If when considering an unusual incident or event, and after exhausting all rational explanation, a weird element remains, that incident, or event and objects pertaining to it, has "medicine."

So, before we decide to take our ghost light medicine, we will dutifully consider whether there are reasonable explanations for the phenomenon or whether our considerations merely serve to emphasize the lights' mysterious nature. For purposes of this discussion it is helpful to compare the cases of the two most famous Texas ghost lights in Marfa and Saratoga. A study and contrast of the two pretty much exhausts the explanations that science offers about the nature and origin of the ghost lights.

The two locations, Marfa and Bragg, could not be more different. Marfa is nearly a mile above sea level. The air there is dry; the rainfall is scant; the vegetation is sparse; and the terrain is desert-like and mountainous. The area epitomizes the Old Southwest range country. Saratoga is less than a hundred feet above sea level. The air there is torrid and humid; the rainfall is abundant; the vegetation is luxuriant; and the terrain is swampy. It is the only place in the nation outside of the Everglades that can legitimately be called jungle country.

The Marfa Lights are seen regularly south of Hwy. 90 about eight miles east of town toward Alpine. So common are sightings that the Texas Highway Department has a sign marking the best vantage point from which to view the lights from the highway. There have been multiple sightings of the lights for generations, and their fame has spread beyond West Texas through extensive media coverage, including the CBS Evening News.

They seem to appear some miles distant from the highway in a basin near the foothills of the Chinati Mountains. From that distance it is difficult to judge their size, but they typically appear low on the horizon and move in unpredictable directions, for perhaps a minute, before disappearing as mysteriously as they appeared. Varying hues of red and blue are commonly reported, and although sometimes only an orangeish-white glow is seen, they are usually very sharply defined and spherical.

The Bragg Road ghost light near Saratoga, as we have discussed, is usually described as a basketball to beachball-sized, very sharply defined, bluish-white sphere. Because of the dense woods of the area, the Bragg Light cannot be viewed from a distant perspective like the Marfa lights. For this reason sightings are limited to open areas like Bragg Road itself and occasionally the pipeline right-of-ways that cross it at two points. This situation and the flat terrain also produce more close-at-hand observations. Unlike the Marfa Lights, it is common for the Bragg Light to be approached by, or to approach, its observers closely, sometimes within a few feet, so that estimates of its size are likely to be reliable. There are variations in the descriptions of the light's behavior and sometimes it is described as being considerably larger than a beach ball and of an orange-white luminosity. The Marfa Lights may involve the successive appearance and disappearance of more than one light or even the appearance of several lights at once, whereas the Bragg Light usually involves the appearance of only one light at the time.

Like the Bragg Light, the Marfa Lights have their counterparts in folklore. In the Trans-Pecos region the Marfa Lights are romantically linked with the spirits of various Mexican revolutionaries or Indian chiefs, particularly that of Chinati, for whom a small mountain range south of Marfa is named.

Skeptics of the Marfa Lights, in an explanation similar to that offered by scoffers of the Bragg Light, reason that the lights are nothing more than the reflections of car lights from the distant Presidio-to-Marfa highway. Others claim that the Bragg Light can be accounted for as fox fire, a phenomenon in which high concentrations of swamp gas or methane are ignited by natural combustion. Although this could be expected to be typical of the Big Thicket, it is difficult to imagine swamp gas in the West Texas desert.

There have been reports from cowboys who work on ranches in the basin that the Marfa Lights have appeared close up and moved directly among them with no cars or other light sources in the vicinity. It would be difficult to attribute this to any subtle trick of optics or to car light beams bouncing off the layers of heat waves in the desert air that, in fact, can sometimes reflect distant light sources at night in a mirage-like phenomenon. As we have already seen, accounts of close encounters with the Bragg Light are not uncommon, including claims that the light has come right up to the windshields of the cars of observers. Some of these up-close encounters, as we have also seen, have resulted in interference and disruption of electrical systems.

The association of ghost lights with abnormally strong electromagnetic conditions has been well documented. This property of the ghost lights, which is dramatically exhibited by accounts from Bragg Road, is present but less documented in the Marfa Lights, due probably to the fact that most sightings of the latter are made from long range. Most researchers assume that the electromagnetic nature of the lights means that they are a little known type of discharge phenomenon resulting from unusual, highly localized recurrent intensifications of the geomagnetic field.

Generally, geophysical forces are assumed to be the source of these conditions with possible contributing meteorological factors. There are a number of known phenomena, produced from these sources, that are commonly appealed to in an attempt to account for the ghost lights. These include, in decreasing order of commonness, lights produced by solar magnetic storms, by stress from earthquake activity along geologic fault lines, by a little known phenomenon called mountain peak discharge (MPD), and by ball lightning, a rare meteorological phenomenon.

It is true that the electromagnetic conditions associated with ghost lights sometimes coincide with solar storms. It is also true, as researchers like Devereux and Persinger have gone to great lengths to demonstrate, that many ghost light locations occur on or near active fault lines, and that both sources are also known to sometimes produce unusual light-forms.

Solar magnetic storms can produce luminosity in the earth's atmosphere such as the Aurora Borealis or Northern Lights. Seismic activity sometimes produces lights, called "earthquake lights," through a process known as the piezoelectric effect in which quartz-bearing rocks emit electrical discharges when subjected to extreme stress.

Ball lightning is a rare phenomenon in which short-lived, spherical light-forms are produced by electrical storms. Particular mountains in such places as Greece, Britain, South America, and the United States have been reported to occasionally emit unusual lights, usually from their peaks, in a phenomenon known as mountain peak discharge. There are, however, difficulties in equating these phenomena with recurrent localized ghost lights, indicating that ghost lights may have a different and more mysterious origin.

Ghost light occurrences are far more frequent than ball lightning and there is no evidence that ball lightning occurrences localize in particular places like ghost lights. Also, ghost lights are known to frequently appear when electrical storms are not present.

Even though quartz-bearing crystals under extreme stress have been shown experimentally to produce luminosity, lights produced by seismic stress more typically exhibit a broadly diffuse glow than the sharply defined spherical shape of the ghost lights. It is also not clear that a piezoelectric discharge along a fault line would be transported to the surface and maintain a discrete, spherical, basketball-sized form for as long as ghost lights are known to manifest.

The theory that seismic activity along fault lines is the lights' cause is at first glance attractive because it would also account for why the lights appear repeatedly in the same locations. Admittedly, many ghost light locations do occur along active fault lines, but there are notable exceptions that do not fit this theory. The Bragg Light occurs in one of the world's most seismically stable areas, in the middle of a vast swampy region with deep alluvial soils where there are no quart-bearing rocks, nor rocks of any kind for that matter, to be subjected to stress and to produce light discharges. Geologically speaking, in fact, the Big Thicket region is little more than a huge half-baked mud pie. This geological model just does not seem to apply to the Bragg Light, and so must be questioned as the ultimate source of the ghost light phenomenon in general.

The very fact that the ghost light phenomenon exists in the present geological conditions of Southeast Texas suggests that, although the lights may sometimes coincide with active fault lines, something other than geological factors must be involved. The sharp contrast between the conditions under which the Marfa and Bragg Lights recur, in fact, is a good illustration of the problems critics have in attributing ghost lights to any geophysically or meteorologically produced phenomena.

The mountain peak discharge phenomenon, which I will abbreviate as MPD, may have some intriguing parallels to some ghost light locations, including the Marfa Lights. It is not a likely explanation for them, however, for all the reasons already discussed that suggest that the ghost lights are not mere discharge phenomena. MPD lights are very short-lived, usually lasting no more than a fraction of a second. Sometimes these lights do assume a spherical shape, but the phenomenon more normally resembles a brief miniature lightning bolt. The MPD phenomenon is highly interesting in its own right, however, and is worth a brief side discussion.

The first time I saw MPD was on a trip with my associates Stan Shaw and Bill Fleming to an area in the Chihuahuan desert of northern Mexico called the "Sierra de Silencio" or "Zone of Silence." This area is so-named because the geomagnetic field there is so highly charged that radio frequency waves will not propagate through the atmosphere. There is a 50,000 watt clear channel radio station in Ciudad Acuna right across the river from Del Rio, Texas, that can be picked up over a vast area of North

America day and night, yet we could not pick it up from less than 200 miles away when we were in the Zone of Silence. Nor could we pick up any other station.

One evening while driving through the Zone, I noticed what looked like strange balls of light and flares shooting off from the peaks of a small mountain range nearby. At first the lights were so faint that I thought it was some kind of optical illusion and that my eyes were playing tricks on me. When I pointed out the lights to Stan and Bill, though, they, too, were seeing them at the same times in the same places. None of us had ever heard of Mountain Peak Discharge at that time, so it was a novel experience.

The drive back to Austin during the twilight and evening hours took us through other mountain ranges that were outside the Zone of Silence. None of them exhibited the phenomenon. It is likely that MPD is related to the unusually intensified magnetic conditions in this Zone of Silence. The area, which is desert-like and very sparsely populated, has a reputation for numerous UFO and other unusual light-form sightings.

Our initial MPD sightings were made from quite some distance, but on another occasion Stan, his son Jeff, and I returned to that area of northern Mexico in an attempt to see the phenomenon close up. We drove deep into the desert mountains about a hundred miles from the nearest town of significant size and fifty miles off the paved highway. Rough jeep trails took us within a few hundred feet of the peaks of the mountains that we hoped would exhibit MPD. We pulled out our cots and sleeping bags near a trail side shrine to the Blessed Virgin Mary and decided to climb to the top of a nearby westward facing ridge to watch the sun set.

We were confident that we had placed ourselves in an ideal position to accomplish our objective, but about an hour before twilight, we were suddenly paid a surprise visit by two truckloads of armed Federal Jurisdiction Police. The Federales parked a couple of hundred feet below us near the shrine and jumped from their vehicles brandishing Uzzis and automatic pistols. Through an interpreter they explained to us that we were suspected of being drug runners, and they accused us of having gone up the hillside to hide our stash.

A few of their agents went up and searched among the boulders where we had been and were not satisfied when they found nothing. The looks on their faces told us they were sure they would nail us when they searched Stan's Bronco. As they were digging through our gear they came across a copy of the *I Ching,* the Chinese Book of Changes. The interpreter examined it closely, and we could just see his wheels grinding to the conclusion that gringos reading such a book must be using dope.

He asked us if it was a book of oriental philosophy. We had no choice but to admit that it was, and we fully expected dope to materialize in the truck, although none of us ever touched the stuff. It seemed inevitable that we would be spending at least a few weeks in a Mexican jail until we could bribe our way out, but then the interpreter replied to our astonishment that his captain had an interest in such things.

The captain approached and I attempted to explain to him in Spanish that we had come to those mountains to study and observe the mysterious power that lies within them. The captain listened very respectfully and then told his men to release us. It turned out that he was an initiate of a Sufi master from India and that the knowledge of places of special power is part of Sufi Tradition.

The captain then told us that the area was a favorite place for drug runners to smuggle their contraband across the border to their Texas compadres. It was very dangerous there, he said, and we should leave immediately. He added that we were very lucky that they found us before the banditos did. Some of the gangs posed as Federal Jurisdiction Police, he said. If they had found us first, they would have shot or beaten us, left us for dead, and stolen the Bronco. As we drove past the shrine on our way out, we couldn't help but think that our good luck, in that this particular company of Federales had a captain who was also a Sufi mystic, bordered on divine intervention.

Thus it was that we did not get to stay and observe MPD among the peaks. That was all the more disappointing because as we were driving out in the gathering darkness we could see the characteristic balls and streaks of light begin to display. This time we were much closer to the peaks than on the previous trip, and we could plainly see the orange-colored balls and streaking discharges with the unaided eye.

Partly through these experiences, I suspected that MPD would be in evidence in the Chinati Mountains near the basin where the Marfa Lights appear. That region of West Texas is part of the Chihuahuan Desert and is virtually contiguous to the Zone of Silence, so it seemed reasonable that it might be subject to similar intense magnetic conditions. If it is, the mountains in the area should also exhibit MPD. I do not suspect that MPD accounts for the Marfa ghost light sightings, however, for the reasons already discussed, but MPD might in some way indicate that the magnetic conditions necessary for the manifestation of genuine ghost lights are present.

My suspicion was confirmed when I participated in a study of the Marfa Lights conducted by Yoshi-Hiko Ohtsuki, a professor of physics at Waseda University of Tokyo. Ohtsuki's study was being documented by the production company of "The Chase," a nationally syndicated show on Japanese television that somewhat resembles the American program "Unsolved Mysteries." The production company invited me to join the project and flew me and

Richard Stewart, a reporter who also documented the project for the *Houston Chronicle,* to the nearest airport at El Paso. During the three-hour drive out to Marfa, I predicted that there would be mountain peak discharge in the nearby Chinatis.

On the first night we were not allowed into professor Ohtsuki's camp, so I suggested that we drive out the Presidio highway to the point nearest Chinati Peak. We arrived there after midnight and the MPD, though not as bright nor as frequently occurring as we had seen in Mexico, was definitely present. Richard would later describe his perception of the lights in his book, *Transparent Tales: An Attic Full of Texas Ghosts,* which he co-authored with fellow veteran *Houston Chronicle* reporter, Allan Turner: "The lights seemed to follow no pattern. Some seemed to tumble down the mountain like falling rocks. Others went up like super-fast mountain goats. Most lasted only an instant, but others shone for several seconds."

Richard had never heard of the MPD phenomenon, and at first thought I had solved the mystery of the Marfa Lights. But there are no mountains in the Big Thicket, I pointed out, so how could he explain the ghost lights that occur there to be merely the product of the MPD phenomenon?

The Marfa and Bragg locations bear virtually no similarities in terms of topography, prevalent weather conditions, mineral content, vegetation or anything that would suggest a common geophysical or meteorological source for such a phenomenon to occur in both locations for generations. It was just this dissimilarity, and the evidence that both ghost lights may be instances of naturally occurring electrical plasmas of an unknown origin that drew the attention of Ohtsuki. The professor, who is also Chairman of the International Committee for Ball Lightning/Fireball Research, is actively involved in studying locations world-wide where these unusual lights occur to determine the variables that result in their manifestation.

Ohtsuki's project obtained photographs of several unusual appearing lights. Through such techniques as spectral analysis and the principles of optics, he demonstrated, not unexpectedly, that most of these lights are, indeed, reflections of car lights and other man-made light sources that bounce off the strata of heat in the desert air. However, he also was satisfied that he had obtained photographs of the genuine article, a spherical fireball of some several inches in diameter.

During this study Ohtsuki spent several weeks at the Marfa Lights location, but was only able to make a short three-day visit to the Bragg Light location. Although he did not obtain a photograph of the Bragg Light, from his study of the area and documented accounts of observers, he concluded that a phenomenon similar to the West Texas ghost lights occurs there.

Significantly, Ohtsuki's interest in the Bragg Light is the fact that, based on his data, there are more sightings of what he calls "fireballs" in Texas than anywhere else in the world. He estimates that on a world-wide average statistically between one and two people per thousand population have witnessed what he considers reliable sightings of fireballs. In the Marfa area, he says, the figure is about eighty in a thousand. The figure for Hardin County would certainly approach, if not exceed, that of Marfa. "In this respect," he told me in conversation, "Texas is very strange. There must be very unusual conditions that contribute to this."

Although he uses the term "ball lightning," Ohtsuki believes the phenomenon may be of a different nature and not necessarily related to electrical storms, the only known source of ball lightning. He favors the theory that the lights result from the electrical charging and resultant ionizing of the aerosol content of the atmosphere in a given area. Aerosol, in the sense that he uses it, refers to microscopic levels primarily of dust, pollen, and moisture that are suspended in the atmosphere. The charge necessary to produce this effect, he theorizes, comes by an unknown process from the local electromagnetic field that is for some reason temporarily excited under extremely localized conditions by some outside source.

The most likely candidate for this outside source of excitation, he believes, are the proton flares produced by massive magnetic storms on the surface of the sun, popularly known as sunspots. That the lights are electrical plasmas, or electrical fires caused by ionization, he feels is evident, and he thinks an understanding of their physics may be of importance in the development of nuclear fusion technology.

By an unknown mechanism, anomalous magnetic conditions may create magnetic "bottles" in which transient miniatures of the fusion reactions that take place on the sun occur in the form of fireballs or ghost lights. Ohtsuki is particularly interested in such recurrent ghost light locations as Marfa and Bragg, since the very fact of the long history of recurrences at such locations indicates the repeated recurrences of the magnetic conditions which theoretically produce them.

The relationship between unusual lights and localized anomalous magnetic conditions associated with sunspot activity has been widely documented. Generally, however, it is assumed that solar magnetic disturbances are the triggering mechanism for seismic or geophysical processes that produce the lights. Ohtsuki's research suggests that solar magnetic disturbances may be more directly causally related, at least with regard to recurrent localized ghost lights, than had been thought.

The fact that ghost lights are known to recur in specific areas and to have done so for indeterminate lengths of time raises an interesting point. If solar activity were the only factor in their manifestation, one would expect that the locations of ghost light appearances would be randomly distributed on the earth's surface. The question then arises; if geophysical considerations such as fault lines, mountain ranges, and mineral deposits do not account for their clustering in specific areas, as our comparison of the Texas ghost lights implies, what could account for it? Specifically, to illustrate the point with the Texas ghost lights, if Marfa and Bragg do not have geophysical features in common, what do they have in common that would suggest a possible common source of their respective lights?

The one thing that they do have in common, which at first might seem only coincidental, is that they occur at almost exactly the same latitude, within a range of about fifteen to twenty miles north of 30 degrees north latitude, allowing for the lights' movements. This is not an isolated coincidence, as ghost lights are reported to occur elsewhere along this same general latitude in Louisiana, Florida, Algeria and Egypt. Similar, though perhaps less recurrent, fireball phenomena have been reported at various times, again at almost this same latitude, near Huffman, Texas, near Gulf Breeze, Florida, and just outside Llano, Texas.

The light near Llano is recurrent enough to be called the Six Mile Light from its proximity to a nearby creek of that name. It is located in the Llano Uplift region, where granite hills are geologically uplifted from deep within the earth, in contrast to the eroded limestone plateau that constitutes the rest of the Central Texas Hill Country. One of these granite hills is the protruding tip of a batholith, known as Enchanted Rock, that is actually a huge shaft that projects 500 feet above the surface. It has not been determined how far it extends below the surface, but some geologists think it may reach all the way to the molten core of the earth.

Mysterious lights have been seen near the rock's summit from time to time. Witnesses include Ira Kennedy, publisher of *Enchanted Rock* magazine, and also the Superintendent of the state park there. The rock is said to have been given its name by the Indians. It is likely that they saw the lights there, since they considered the rock to be a sacred place.

The latitude correlation with the ghost lights apparently extends outside the United States. Upon hearing this information, Ohtsuki noted with interest that there is a well known ghost light location in the small islands at the extreme southern tip of Japan at about 30 degrees north latitude. Some of the points on the alignment indicated can be connected by what is virtually a straight line, and their alignment may indicate the presence of a trans-global line of geomagnetic force. The slight variations of a straight line of the points might be expected of a line of energy that would probably be of a helical or wave pattern form. It is known that extremely low frequencies (ELF) of the earth's electromagnetic field, because they have such long wavelengths, are capable of encircling the earth. Could there be such lines of energy that somehow attract the magnetic disturbances of the sun, causing localized excitation of the magnetic field, consistent with Ohtsuki's theory, and causing the ghost lights?

If there are such lines of force that attract energy from the sunspots, why would only particular spots along such lines be subject to the production of the magnetic anomalies that apparently induce the lights? Are ghost light locations that are not situated on 30 degrees north latitude part of other alignments of places with unusual magnetic conditions? These questions are presently unanswered.

For the moment it's important to recognize that there are factors involved in the ghost lights that do not conform to simple geological, seismological, or meteorological causal models. Mineral deposits in mountains, earthquake activity, and unusual forms of lightning simply do not account for the ghost lights' existence. There have to be other factors involved, and some of these, as we will see, may stretch the envelope of our most basic ideas about how the Universe works, and about the structure of space itself.

You may be convinced by now that such lights are not the stuff of fairy tales and constitute a genuine unknown; Ohtsuki's work at least has established this much. In case you're thinking that these lights and the disturbances that cause them are insignificant and are wondering what relevance this has to anyone but to those of us who have an interest in bizarre phenomena, you should be aware that the effects carry beyond the immediate ghost light locations. Recurrent electrical disturbances may sometimes affect much larger areas than the specific locations where the lights occur and may have the same kinds of dramatic effects as the ghost lights. Reports of unusual TV and radio reception or interference and the mysterious dimming or blackout of domestic electrical facilities have been observed in the areas of the Hornet Spook Light and the Yakima Indian Reservation light, for example.

In some cases the areas involved may affect hundreds of thousands of people all of whom are unconsciously subjected to these unusual energies. This illustrates the importance of understanding the subtle forces involved in mystery light phenomena and the means by which they impact and interact with living organisms. These energies may have a disturbing impact on the human mind. It is profoundly in our interests that we be aware of the mechanism and its possible effects on consciousness. To illustrate the potential extent of the widespread effects of these disturbances consider the following excerpts from an article in the May 3, 1985 edition of the *Beaumont Enterprise* by Kevin Carmody:

"Skeptics questioning how lightning in Arkansas could have caused Wednesday's blackout spanning Southeast Texas and Southwest Louisiana might want to consider how bizarre the alternative explanations are.

"Ruling out UFOs, sabotage and nuclear attack, you'd be left with: an electromagnetic disturbance of incredible proportion. 'It is rare and it's unlikely than an electromagnetic interruption could be of that magnitude, but it is theoretically possible,' says Larry Mansueiti, staff engineer for the American Public Power Association.

"But such an occurrence might have coincided with the peak of the blackout, at about 12:30 a.m. to 1:30 a.m. At that time, Gulf States Utilities engineers acknowledged that they were as much in the dark about the cause of the blackout as the 132,000 customers were literally.

"Some Beaumont residents who didn't lose power reported picking up Houston television stations; others noticed unusual fluctuations of radio station signals. And a *Beaumont Enterprise* photographer picked up two-way radio transmissions traveling three or four times their normal range. All that would be consistent with a localized disturbance in the electromagnetic field surrounding the earth.

"But other phenomena reported included power surges in electrical systems of cars—similar to the type of disruption than can cause a utility transmission line to overload. 'If a transmission line is running at capacity, it is possible that an extremely powerful electromagnetic disturbance could trip a relay, which Gulf States engineers say is what happened,' Mansueiti said. 'The next question is what caused it, and that's a much more difficult question to answer.'

"Mansueiti said the most common cause of electromagnetic disruption would be sun spots, or solar storms.'…sun spot disturbances normally have a wider effect, but if one is narrowly focused on one spot, it might be strong enough,' he said."

Representatives of Gulf States Utilities officially stuck by their theory that a lightning storm about a hundred miles north of Beaumont had blown out a transformer and tripped a relay resulting in the blackout. Reporter Kevin Carmody didn't buy this explanation. He happened to have been out the night of the blackout. He had been working late at the paper and was on his way home at about 1:00 a.m. when he decided to drop by the automatic teller machine at his bank not far from downtown to make a withdrawal. He was sitting in his car in the ATM drive-through lane with the engine running and the car's lights on at precisely the time the blackout hit Beaumont. It was not raining and there was absolutely no lightning in evidence anywhere in the area. Suddenly somebody turned the lights out. The bank building's lights, the street lights, traffic signals and the lights of other buildings and homes for as far as he could see were instantly plunged into an eerie darkness. Then suddenly his car's engine went dead and its lights went out. He struggled to restart his car to no avail. Its battery had suddenly and mysteriously gone dead. A few minutes later, however, he was able to restart the car. The radio, which had also been blacked out, came back to life but crackled and hissed with interference.

You can readily see why Carmody did not accept the lightning theory of the utility company and why he bothered to dig a little deeper into the cause of the blackout. The fact that his car had gone dead had not been a coincidence. Whatever knocked out the utility grid also knocked out his car, and it was obvious that lightning a hundred miles away could have had nothing to do with his car's blackout.

I'd have given a week's pay to have been on Bragg Road that night in May of 1985. The prospects of seeing the light would probably have been very good. Just before he left Beaumont to take a new job in Washington, D.C., Kevin Carmody told me that when he got back to work the next morning he found that the

Enterprise had received numerous reports that night of car engine failures, unusual radio and television interference and reception, and of strange lights streaking through the early morning sky.

William, a former classmate of mine who asked not to be further identified, was in mid-level management for Gulf States at their corporate offices in Beaumont at the time of the blackout, so I had lunch with him one day to see what he knew about this occurrence. He pretty much repeated the company line about lightning being the cause of the blackout, despite the evidence to the contrary of Carmody's article. There was one curious aspect to the story he had heard, though, that he admitted seemed a little odd. He had heard reports that a large black cat of some kind had been linked to the transformer failure that the company officially maintained was the cause of the blackout.

It wasn't clear to him exactly what role the black cat had played. Some said that its proverbial curiosity fried the cat when it examined some of the utility's equipment a little too closely, and this had contributed to the equipment's failure. William doubted this, but he thought it likely that there had been a notable encounter of some kind with an actual black cat and that it was probably someone's sense of humor or sense of the ironic that perpetuated the company rumors. From what we will see in a later chapter, the association of a large black cat with a mysterious power failure may be more than just an amusingly coincidental and quaint reminder of our superstitious past.

It may be just such spots, where solar magnetic disturbances are apparently temporarily focused for as yet unknown reasons, that we are dealing with in the ghost light sightings locations. This would raise the obvious question, having already seen that geological, meteorological, and seismological considerations do not seem to be the determining factors, of why such disturbances would tend to focus recurrently on the same spots. But in all these considerations are we really dealing with what actually causes ghost lights? Are we to assume that an understanding of their electromagnetic aspect would explain their origin and nature?

Even if ghost lights are assumed to be purely of an electromagnetic nature, it is not clear by what process the actual form of the lights could be produced, or be maintained for as long as many that have been observed. The lights are typically perfect spheres, even when moving at considerable speed, and are usually of about the same diameter no matter where they occur. They have been observed for prolonged periods of up to five minutes or more.

There are no known principles of physics or electrodynamics to adequately explain the ghost lights. It is not likely, then, that ghost lights are a mere electrical discharge phenomenon, no matter what might be their hypothetical energy source, and there may be no direct causative link with any fully understood form of energy. About all that can be said in this regard with any degree of certainty is that ghost lights are statistically associated with intense electromagnetic disturbances that are recurrent in particular highly localized areas. Ohtsuki's research and Carmody's remarkable experience seem to support solar magnetic storms or sunspots as the most likely outside source of the energy of these disturbances. It may be that these electromagnetic conditions merely provide a medium for the lights' appearances.

To say that these conditions are the cause of the lights might be as naive as our ancestors' belief that fly larvae are generated spontaneously by filth and putrefaction. Researcher Paul Devereux realized this and said of the association of ghost lights with intensified electromagnetic conditions that, "This dawn of realization regarding the conditions that frame their appearance, however, does not tell us what the lights actually are."

Not only are the lights physically a mystery, but so is their observed behavior. The lights' movements, their bobbing and weaving, and their dance-like acrobatics do not seem to be merely mechanical responses to physical forces. They are more suggestive of playfulness. Several of the researchers already cited report that at times the lights seem to interact with their observers, sometimes approaching or even chasing them, and sometimes receding from and eluding them. Frequently, after prolonged periods of such behavior, the lights will streak away far into the distance in an instant, leaving incredulous witnesses with the uncanny feeling that they have been both observed and played with, and suggesting the unthinkable—that the lights appear to act consciously. Our friend Jim, whose story began this account, would certainly not argue with this observation, no matter how difficult to accept it might be for someone who has not had a similar experience.

It is not uncommon for witnesses to comment that the lights seemed intelligent, seemed to play with them, or even appeared to be smarter than their observers in a kind of game of hide and seek. Such testimony, however, is largely anecdotal and of an admittedly subjective nature. It is thus difficult for most researchers to grant consciousness to the lights. They are, however, sufficiently impressed by such accounts and the inadequate physical models to come up with some fairly exotic theories of what the lights might be and of what they might represent.

Researcher David Clarke speculates that the lights are evidence of what he calls "an energy form on the very margin of physical existence." This aspect of the energy, he says, "makes it sensitive to consciousness." Devereux theorizes that the lights may be some form of life, but of their broader implication he says, "I continue to feel that we are dealing with a very sensitive energy form, sufficiently sensitive to react to consciousness itself." He further theorizes that the energy of the lights might challenge our mechanistic view that consciousness is a product of the brain, and that the lights may be some form of incorporeal consciousness. He says, "In my opinion we need to start thinking of consciousness as a field effect, an all-pervading element in the universe, perhaps associated with space-time in ways not currently apparent to us, and affected by the presence of electromagnetism and mass."

In the ghost lights we face a mystery in the original meaning of the word as something that is both hidden and revealed. The general locations of the lights' appearances are known, and there is a more than reasonable expectation that they will appear again. They are at least partially of an electromagnetic nature, so even though their precise origin and nature are unknown, they can be studied to some extent within the framework of what is known. As such the lights may well represent genuine incursions of the Unknown into what we regard as the known reality.

In all of this we may simply be struggling with our modern materialistic bias toward a new appreciation of what our ancestors have long taken as self-evident. Traditional cultures all over the world have regarded ghost lights as conscious beings and as evidence of a non-physical reality that at times interacts with our own. The ancient Celts believed that at certain times in particular places the boundary between this and other worlds grows thin, allowing denizens of other realities access to this one. There is evidence that they and other cultures associated these occurrences with the ebb and flow of terrestrial magnetism and its relation to lunar and solar influences. They placed much emphasis on predicting when and where these energies would reach peak intensities.

We are perhaps prejudiced in our tendency to dismiss such traditions as naive or pre-scientific because they associate the lights with fairies, demons, ghosts, and spirits. Were we able to look at the phenomenon more objectively, the lights might well

have much to teach us about the possibilities of conscious participation in a greater universe of which what we now take to be the
whole of reality is but a small part.

If after reading this account you are of a mind to head for one
of the ghost light locations discussed here to see one of the lights
for yourself, you should be forewarned. Although most sightings
of the lights pass without serious incident, and many of them, like
the Marfa Lights, can be seen from a safe distance, this is not
always the case. Consider the experiences that have been related
of the Bragg Light witnesses. Anything that is capable of blacking
out a car's electrical systems should certainly be approached with
caution. And aside from the danger of physical harm there is a
more subtle consideration.

If you go stalking the Bragg Light you should not assume that
you will return with your sense of reality intact. The long displaced Indians of Southeast Texas are said to have avoided the
Big Thicket, especially its depths in that part of Hardin County
where the ghost light has been seen for so many years. They
believed those ancient, shadowy woods to be the haunt of evil
spirits and demons. But if you do not share their version of reality
that would allow for such things, and if you will not heed their
foreboding, consider the testimony of our old friend Jim, whose
story began this narrative. His personal reality map was altered so
severely, by what he had no doubt was a living thing, that it was
over thirty years before he could bring himself to even talk to anyone about it.

From this account you may now agree that ghost lights constitute a compelling and genuine unknown. In cases like Jim's,
though, where witnesses attest to the apparent conscious behavior
of the lights, you may still suspect that the witnesses are only
overreacting out of fear to an unknown that merely needs more
study. That might be a reasonable observation if what has been

presented so far were all there is to the mystery, but the ghost lights themselves are only part of a much greater mystery.

The ghost lights as they have been described–as basketball-sized spheres that appear recurrently in the same general locations–are not the only unusual light-forms that are seen regularly in the highly localized areas where intense periodic magnetic fluxes are known to occur. Two other types of lights are seen, although less frequently and in less predictable and specific locations.

Large, orange-colored fireballs have been seen on a number of occasions in the Bragg Road area and in other places in Southeast Texas. At times they have been observed at ground level, and at times moving relatively slowly through the air. When seen airborne, witnesses sometimes at first mistake them for the face of the full moon. At least one has been seen actually on Bragg Road itself and was close up enough for the witness to estimate that it was about thirty feet across.

I witnessed this type of light over thirty years ago while on the way from Sour Lake to Beaumont. There were four of us in the car headed almost due east. Shortly after sunset, the fireball appeared in the northeast, traveled over a considerable arc of the sky, and disappeared below the woods on the horizon to the southeast. It was impossible to know how large or distant the object was, but we had a sense that this was not a shooting star or meteor. It seemed much closer.

Years later this suspicion was confirmed when I learned of someone who had witnessed a similar, if not identical, event during the same time frame from further south, near the town of Fannett. To her it appeared that the light disappeared on the northwestern horizon. Apparently the light had actually landed at some point between where I had seen it and where the lady from Fannett saw it. I also learned that a similar event, again during the same time frame, had been witnessed by several other people from Sour Lake.

One or more of the fireballs in question might have landed in the vicinity of a place known as Big Hill near Fannett, from what Melvin Jones, a friend of my sister, Shannon Dow, told us. Melvin's grandfather was a rice farmer whose normal routine was to arrive at his fields just before dawn. One morning, he needed to go to work early to complete some tasks left undone from the day before. At about 3:00 a.m., as he approached his farm near Big Hill, he suddenly found himself accompanied by a huge ball of light, about 20 feet in diameter, that moved down the road alongside his pick-up. The intense, orange-colored light illuminated the interior of his truck briefly before it passed him and disappeared in the direction of Big Hill. Big Hill is named after a modest rise caused by a salt dome that penetrates the surface of the surrounding prairie and marsh. Such hills are about the only breaks in the otherwise featureless coastal plains that lie just south of the Big Thicket.

This story calls to mind the lore of the trooping fairies, as reported by Ted Holiday and Jacques Vallee among others, in relation to UFO research. The fairies were said to gather in large troops as they returned to their homes after a night of carousing and mischief-making. To human observers the troops were said to resemble large fireballs, and the fairies were said to have made their homes in hills. Those who inadvertently wandered near the fairy hills are said to have sometimes been able to hear their bawdy merry making from within the hills, and sometimes to have been abducted or to have gone mad. Melvin's grandfather apparently survived his encounter all right, but there is another story that might be relevant here about someone who might not have been that fortunate.

A high school classmate of my parents frequently fished on the Pine Island Bayou south of Sour Lake and back downstream toward Beaumont. He would spend days at a time running trotlines out of his fish camp on the bayou's edge. On one of his outings he came across a mysterious cylindrical object in the woods. He couldn't tell whether it was made of metal, stone, some kind of concrete, or whether it was an artifice of some kind or was naturally occurring. He attempted to mark the location of the object so he could come back later and attempt to identify it.

He was unable to relocate the object. For years he made repeated trips to the bayou. Eventually no one paid any attention to his story. His persistent efforts to rediscover whatever he saw obsessed him to the point of insanity, and he lived out the rest of his days demented, incapable of maintaining a coherent conversation and unable to live a normal life. The stretch of the bayou where he fished was on the line where the fireballs were seen.

From a group of young men who also had a fishing camp on the Pine Island Bayou, I heard of a large, orange fireball sighting that took place 30 years later. Their camping trips usually involved staying up late and running a trotline as their method of fishing. One night they left their camp to go to town to replenish their supplies. Just as they arrived back at the camp, a large spherical light about 25 to 30 feet in diameter slowly ascended from the floor of the forest, hovered briefly just above the treetops, and then streaked away. Again, the boys' campsite would have been in the approximate area where the fireball my friends and I saw on the way to Beaumont disappeared over the horizon.

Other lights that are seen are apparently at considerable altitude, although a lack of perspective makes it impossible to estimate their size or distance from observers. At first they appear to be ordinary stars, although a bit larger and brighter than average. What makes it obvious that they are not ordinary stars is that they move in patterns that trace geometrical shapes. Typically, such a light will move in a straight line across a considerable arc of the night sky; abruptly make a right angle turn without slowing down; trace another line at a perpendicular to the first one; and then trace the diagonal between the end points of the two lines.

The lights will also trace rectangular and triangular patterns. These maneuvers, the distances they cover, and their speeds would be impossible for known aircraft. The movements of the lights are suggestive of signaling and are reminiscent of the playfulness and acrobatic movements sometimes reported of ghost lights. Could it be that these aerial stunts are intended for the eyes of observers? That was the feeling I got when I saw them.

I was working one summer during my college years for my uncle, Bud Poss, who was the greens superintendent for a local golf course. My job was to double as the night watchman and to move the sprinkler heads on the course's irrigation system back before they had automatic sprinklers. The golf course was in a newly developed area carved from a portion of the southern end of the Big Thicket and is bisected by the Little Pine Island Bayou. The holes on the outward nine, before they turned back toward the clubhouse, were still surrounded at the time by dense woods. One moonless and particularly dark night, while I was out moving the sprinkler heads on the fairway of the hole that was farthest from the clubhouse, I was witness to the lights' performing in the manner described. My first reaction, after the astonishment of realizing that the lights were not normal stars, was to be afraid, but as I watched in amazement, an almost overwhelming eerie feeling gave way to fascination and wonder.

Some two decades later, while conducting my research in the Saratoga area, a gentleman described a light performing the same kinds of acrobatics near the West Hardin High School. He and several others saw it clearly from one of the ball fields on the school's campus, and they all agreed that it could not have been a star or any kind of aircraft they knew about.

All of these large fireball and moving star-like lights in Hardin County were seen within a relatively small area and within 20 to 30 miles of one another. The sightings have occurred over an extended period of at least 30 to 40 years. In each case the observers were unknown to one another and none realized that anyone else had experienced anything similar on other occasions.

Under these circumstances patterns are not discerned and invariably the sightings are dismissed or are lightly regarded by anyone other than the witnesses. Without the knowledge that others have had similar experiences the witnesses themselves may even be left doubting their own experiences. If the Big Thicket area was the only place where such lights have been seen regularly over a period of decades, you might question whether they constitute enough information to establish a pattern.

Within the last ten years, the star-like lights moving in geometrical patterns have also been seen by independent witnesses in the skies above Cedar Mountain in Llano County, Texas. This is in the same area where the Six Mile Light appears and where mysterious lights have been seen on the summit of Enchanted Rock. As noted earlier, both of these locations occur on approximately the same latitude as the Marfa Lights and the Bragg Light.

One prominent researcher of paranormal phenomena, John Keel, claims to have detected a pattern in the order in which these lights manifest. The sequence goes like this: First the stars that move in geometrical patterns show up; next the large fireballs are seen streaking slowly from horizon to horizon and on or near the ground; then the smaller spheres known as ghost lights appear.

Keel notes that these same unusual light-form phenomena tend to recur in the same areas over long cycles of time of an undetermined periodicity. He calls these places "window areas." Many years of on-site field research of such places have lead him to the conclusion that the various lights constitute successive phases of manifestation of the same basic phenomenon.

Devereux describes two additional light phenomena that recur in several ghost light locations in Great Britain. These lights might constitute even further stages of the phases of manifestation that Keel noted. Devereux states that, "vaguely human-like, anthropomorphic shapes are reportedly glimpsed within the light energy," and further reports that, "sometimes the lights themselves can take on such forms." The lights seen in such cases are typically what he calls columns of gaseous materials or vaporous luminescent columns. The figures are sometimes seen within the marbling of the cloud-like luminous mists.

Significantly, in at least some of the same areas where anthropomorphic forms are seen within the vaporous lights, smaller lights, "have been seen in the branches of trees," and, pin-points of light," have been observed hovering at a height of ten to fifteen feet. The tell-tale electronic failures typical of ghost light locations are also reported in these areas. My associates and I have observed these "pin-point" lights on two different occasions in the Big Thicket, confirming Devereux's observations. We documented one of these episodes with photographs.

Bill Fleming and I took a photograph on Bragg Road (viewable on our website at www.mysteriousdimension.com) in February 1996. What appears to be a small bluish-white speck at the left center of the road bed was a peculiar light that I at first assumed was a firefly or some other kind of bioluminescent insect. This seemed a bit suspicious, however, since it was far too early in the year for fireflies to be in season. It was also suspicious that there was only one light. When fireflies are out, there is usually a multitude of them present at any one location at a given time.

This light also seemed to be aware of our presence and hovered directly over our heads for about an hour at treetop level, moving in and out of tree branches much in the manner of the British pin-point lights described by Devereux. It then moved down the road about 25 to 50 yards ahead of us and began to move down vertically to within about 10 feet of ground level, and then would return to treetop level. This process was repeated for some time before the light disappeared. Other factors suggested it was not a firefly: it seemed much larger, its color seemed bluer than the typical greenish firefly light, and it seemed to stay "on" much longer than is typical of a firefly.

We contacted Riley Nelson, an entomologist at the University of Texas, and described the light to him. He discounted the likelihood of its having been a firefly for the very reasons that we had been suspicious, but he said that there was some possibility that it could have been a species of Click Beetle native to East Texas. Unless there had been a prolonged warm period during the winter, though, the date of our sighting had been far too early for this species to have been present. Nelson was well aware of the biological diversity of the Thicket and took our account quite seriously. He acknowledged that an exhaustive entomological survey of the Big Thicket could prove to be very interesting.

In any case, Nelson conceded the possibility that we had observed an unusual or little known bioluminescent life form. He could scarcely have suspected how unusual it might prove to be. About two months after seeing this light we returned to the Thicket in the vicinity of Bragg Road when the fireflies were out. There were thousands of them moving about randomly, paying us little heed and sometimes even landing on us. Despite several attempts we were unable to obtain any photographs of them while they were lit up and in the air, even from within a few feet, using the same camera we had used to obtain the photograph in question.

The lights alone constitute a considerable mystery, but Keel does not stop there. After the full sequence of light manifestations, mysterious beings or unusual, out-of-place animals sometimes appear in the window areas. Keel thinks these creatures are manifestations of the same energy that produces the various types of lights. These include large, black cat-like animals. My awareness of this fact made William's account of the black cat rumors circulating at Gulf States Utilities and associating it with the cause of the great Beaumont Blackout hauntingly familiar.

The most common of these mysterious animals is a large, foul-smelling, hairy hominid or ape-like creature, a full discussion of which follows in the next chapter. I must suggest, however, that the firefly or pinpoint lights and the luminous mists that Devereux mentions may constitute further intermediary phases of Keel's progression of energy manifestations that would occur between the ghost lights and the mystery creatures. The photograph on the back cover may provide documentation of this fact.

Bill and I took this picture on January 20, 1996 on Bragg Road. After a number of unsuccessful attempts to obtain a picture of the ghost light, either because it did not appear or because there was not adequate time to take the photo, we decided to make another attempt using a technique we had heard about used in a study of the ghost light at Joplin, Missouri. The theory is that the energy that produces the lights can sometimes exist at a frequency below the visible light spectrum and can be picked up by film even though it is not visible to the naked eye. A standard 35 mm camera with 1000 ASA speed film, we had heard, is all that we needed, and no special photographic equipment would be necessary.

Even operating with this theory, it would have been difficult for us to choose an exact location along the eight mile length of the road to try to get pictures of the light. But as luck would have it, not long after arriving at the entrance of the Ghost Road, we were to have this decision made for us. After driving about three and a half miles from the south entrance, we saw a distinct bluish-white sphere move slowly from east to west about a quarter to a half mile ahead of us.

Although we did not know for sure whether this was a sighting of the genuine mystery light, it was only the second time in some 20 years of hunting the light that I had seen a sphere with such specific characteristics. We proceeded to the spot where we could best estimate that it crossed the road and set up our equipment.

We used no flash in order to avoid the possibility of any kind of light reflection affecting the results. We took several shots with a flash as a test against anything that might show up on a non-flash exposure to be able to compare the respective backgrounds. The light from the flash reflected brightly off the trunk of the pine tree and off the shrubbery surrounding the pine tree. It also sharply illuminated the vines and branches around the tree all the way down to ground level and for a considerable distance on either side of the tree. (This photograph may be seen on our web-site at www.mysteriousdimension.com.)

Only one exposure taken without a flash developed. It looks like fog or smoke, but the weather at the time this exposure was taken was clear and very cold. Temperatures were in the 20s Fahrenheit. There was virtually no humidity and there was absolutely no trace of ground fog or smoke. Even if there had been fog or smoke, we would have had to use a flash to capture it on film.

Technicians at the Holland Photography lab in Austin told us that if this had been fog or smoke, the light would have reflected back into the camera lens and would have whited out the expo-sure, just like a car's headlight high beam will reflect back in dense fog. They also pointed out that in areas of the picture where there was no fog, the flash would have lit up the background the way it did in the test photo taken with a flash. Since this did not happen, the only logical conclusion, they said, is that the vapor or fog shown in this picture is self-luminous and provides the illumination that reveals the contents of the rest of the photograph.

The implications of this analysis suddenly dawned on one of the technicians and he asked me wide-eyed what the hell this was and weren't we scared when we saw it. I had to admit I had no idea what it was, except that it might be what people call a ghost light. The reason we weren't afraid when we took the picture is that at no time was the vapor ever visible to us. For all we knew we were just taking a picture of pitch-black darkness, like all the other exposures that didn't come out at all.

This photograph helps document the existence of the luminescent vapors or mists that Devereux's research has turned up. Since we obtained this photograph, some kids we interviewed on Bragg Road one night told us of a glowing, fog-like mist they had seen on a number of occasions; there was a bright spot in the fog that looked at first glance like someone carrying a very strong flashlight in a dense fog bank. We later learned of another witness who claimed to have seen a similar mist with a bright spot and that the mist "collapsed" into the bright spot and transformed itself into the brilliant sphere that is typical of most sightings. Neither of these witnesses knew of our photograph, nor did they know of each other's accounts.

The fact that the luminous mist in our photograph was not visible to us may support the notion that some stages of the lights' manifestations apparently occur outside the visible light spectrum. But the witness accounts further suggest that the luminous fog stage of the light's manifestation can also occur within the visible light range, and that the luminous fog stage perhaps immediately precedes the brilliant sphere stage.

What is even more interesting is Paul Devereux's report that witnesses have sometimes seen anthropomorphic forms within the marbling of the vapors, and that some have suggested that this was preliminary to human-like forms actually manifesting outwardly from within the glowing mists. If the glowing vapors of which Devereux writes are duplicated on the Ghost Road, could the wild man sightings on the Ghost Road, which I will recount in the next chapter, be related to these human-like forms?

During the course of this research I had occasion to visit the headquarters of the Big Thicket National Preserve in Beaumont. The Preserve is administered by the National Park Service and the park officials there were very cooperative and helpful when they learned that I was writing a book concerning the Big Thicket. They, of course, had all heard of the ghost light on Bragg Road, but I didn't know how they would react to other aspects of my research. Two of the rangers invited me to the library where in conversation I began to hint at some of the strange phenomena of the Big Thicket that I had been investigating.

Not only were they receptive, but the Preserve's chief of resources and education, Bob Valen, began to knowledgeably discuss the possible existence of paranormal phenomena and the implications of theoretical physics that might predict them. He seemed to be testing me to see whether I might think he was weird. When he saw that I was pleased that someone in an official capacity with the Preserve was sympathetic to my research, he began to relate some of the strange experiences of his years with the Park Service.

Bob is a certified Wildland Fire Information Officer. In the Spring of 1996, while stationed at the Big Thicket Preserve, he was assigned temporary duty to cover a forest fire in the Carson National Forest not far from Taos, New Mexico. The U.S. Forest Service names forest fires much the same way hurricanes are named. This 10,000 acre fire was called the Hondo fire.

What was assumed to have been smoke from the forest fire was photographed by one of the forest rangers. Bob saw this remarkable photograph for himself. In the marbling of the smoke, Bob said, were the unmistakable features of the face of a man. The photograph was so remarkable that someone had the good sense to take it to a shaman of the local Native Americans. The face in the smoke, the shaman declared, was manifested by the spirit of a member of an ancient tribe, and the fact that it had appeared was of great portent.

After hearing Bob's story, I showed him the photograph of the self-luminous fog. I detailed to him the same information that you have just read about how we obtained the photograph and then asked him, like I will now ask you to do, to turn the photograph one quarter rotation to the right such that the left-hand side becomes the top. Move it back or step back a few feet and try to look at the entire picture without focusing on any details.

Bob saw it immediately. There is a face forming within the vapor. Emerging from its billows are the features of a creature that is seen in wild places world-wide. Most Native American traditions would refer to it as one of the "Ancient Ones." In the Big Thicket it is called the "Wild Man."

CHAPTER 3

The Wild Man

Abig, hairy, human-like creature of a mysterious nature has been seen periodically in the Big Thicket for generations. Sightings date back at least to the early days of European settlement and probably to the unrecorded past of the Native Americans. Witnesses have variously described it as a "wild man," "an ape-like critter," or a "raggedy man."

The first I heard of the Big Thicket's Wild Man was in the mid-1950s as a ten-year-old boy growing up in Sour Lake. My grandpa had been planning for weeks to take me and my older brother, Mickey, on an overnight camping and fishing trip. Just days before we were to leave, rumors began flying around Hardin County that a wild man, wearing no clothes, but covered with hair, had been seen in the northern part of the county in the dense bottom land forests along Village Creek—the very place we intended to go.

Naturally, we would have been reluctant to go camping on Village Creek under the circumstances, so our mother conspired with our grandpa to conceal the rumor from us until after we had made the trip.

After about an hour's drive that seemed considerably longer to us kids, we arrived at the sand bar that extended across the creek from beneath the old wooden bridge at the McNeely Settlement. As we unfolded our net to seine the cold, spring-fed waters for minnows to use as bait, we met another fisherman who immediately began to warn us about the wild man who had been seen in those parts recently. As the stranger's story unfolded and our concern became apparent, Grandpa just laughed and asked us where our courage was and what had happened to our spirit of adventure. His attitude was that if there were a wild man in those woods, we should like nothing better than to get to see him and just go right up to him and say howdy.

I didn't sleep a bit that night on Village Creek. The hoot of every owl and the croak of every bullfrog announced the imminent arrival of the hairy creature to my overactive imagination. Mickey lay sleepless on his cot most of the night as a shadow cast in the moonlight by a stump on the creek bank took on monstrous form. I was dead certain the wild man had gotten the jump on us when a razorback hog noisily rooted into our camp in the wee hours.

I admit that as we made our way back to town and our familiar routines the next day, I was a little disappointed not to have seen the wild man. I began to wonder, as a child who had just figured out that there is no Santa Claus, whether this wasn't just another boogieman fairy tale.

A few days later, still relishing our adventure, I realized something. Grandpa had laughed and joked about our chances of having an encounter with the weird wild man, but not once had he dismissed the possibility of it actually happening. So I approached him and asked him pointblank if he had just been joking with us to make the trip more fun, like telling ghost stories in the woods around the campfire. Did he really believe it was possible that there could be something as strange and mysterious as a naked, hairy wild man in the Big Thicket?

He recalled that he had heard the wild man stories from time to time and that he thought there must be some basis to them. People said the wild man was an escaped convict who had managed to survive in the woods eating wild berries and armadillos, or a crazy old hermit who delighted in scaring people, or a mental patient who couldn't adapt to normal society but had somehow evolved the survival skills necessary to make the Big Thicket his asylum.

Grandpa thought these were not likely explanations, though. No doubt, there could be convicts and hermits and the like holed up in those woods—the Thicket has a long history of being a hide-out for outlaws and a refuge for reprobates and anti-social types. But nobody—no matter how crazy or desperate or wily— could survive for long in the snake-infested, mosquito-swarmed depths of the Thicket, with its impenetrable brush and thorny vine of every description, with no clothes on. And that is how the wild man was always described—as naked. And then there was the question of the hair. The wild man was always described as being very hairy, apparently noticeably hairier than its startled witnesses would expect of a normal man.

The sightings were typically brief glimpses caught from a moving car before the alleged wild man easily concealed himself in the thick woods that border virtually every country road in the county. Accounts varied as to the wild man's exact appearance, but there was a general agreement that, as reported by the *Kountze News* on August 14, 1952, "...the man had a heavy beard and a hairy body."

Accusations of a hoax quite naturally arose as the *Kountze News* article further reported, "There was speculation as to whether some person was playing a trick. However, reports of a naked 'wild' man in the east Texas woods have been heard from time to time during the last two or three years."

It never occurred to my grandfather that the wild man reports were only hoaxes. It had been seen by hunters who had enough experience in the woods to know when they're seeing something unusual. That was enough to convince him, since he considered himself a member of that fraternity, that and the fact that the

Hardin County Sheriff's Office thought enough of the reports to investigate the sites of at least some of them. Apparently some of the results of these investigations were noteworthy to the Sheriff's Department because the article also mentioned that the sheriff had said that "…the barefoot tracks were plain in each case."

But after all these more or less rational considerations, my grandpa ended our conversation with an admission of wonder. He had never seen the wild man, but he thought it very likely that the stories were based on something genuinely strange that people occasionally glimpsed. While on hunting trips he had heard the screaming of panthers at night. Stories of screaming black "panthers" (accounts of which are to follow) were legendary in Thicket country, and he knew the so-called experts denied that any such animal even existed or that any kind of panther ever screamed or that any kind of panther that once had actually inhabited the Thicket still existed there. He was familiar with all these expert opinions, but he also knew that his own experience contradicted them.

"The Big Thicket is a mysterious place," he told me. "There are things in those woods people don't know nothin' about." That conversation and the look on my grandfather's face as he spoke those words have always remained vivid in my mind, and my appreciation of the mystery contained within the ancient swamps and forests of the Big Thicket has never waned. But it wasn't until some two decades later that I began to fully appreciate the depth of that mystery.

In 1979 I was working as associate editor of the *Kountze News* for Buddy Moore. The folklore of Thicket country had naturally always interested me, and I undertook to write a series of articles for the paper on the famous Ghost Light of Bragg Road. I had only recently become aware of the thesis by Michael Persinger and Gyslaine Lafreniere on the sources and effects of such lights, and I was intrigued to learn that they had documented and studied ghost light locations over the length and breadth of North America.

The tales I had heard as a child took on a new tone. It was indeed likely that there were genuinely strange goings-on in the Big Thicket, and the folklore of the area was not that of an isolated population of Southern backwoods rustics, but seemed to fit a pattern suggestive of a global enigma. What was particularly intriguing was that researchers Persinger and Lafreniere had also documented the appearance of mystery creatures such as large, hairy ape-like humanoids and large black cats in the same areas where the ghost lights were known to occur. I had often wondered if there were any relation between the Bigfoot legends of the Northwest and the wild man stories from Southeast Texas, and their research made it seem likely that there was a connection. The fact that they had documented periodic sightings of wild man-type hairy creatures in places with long traditions of ghost light appearances led me to believe that the stories coming from the Thicket were genuine. Little did I suspect how bizarre the connection between the lights and the hairy wild man may really be.

My series of articles on the Bragg Light was enthusiastically received, so I decided to find out if any of my readers had any memory of the wild man stories that had circulated some twenty years earlier. Some of them might have even been witnesses and might provide valuable information in studying these puzzling phenomena. With this in mind I invited the readership to inform me of any unusual things they may have seen in the area. The solicitation was very generally stated, and made no reference to the earlier wild man sightings so as not to prejudice or affect any potential responses. The responses I received far exceeded anything I could have imagined, and were stranger than anything I could have made up.

A lady from Kountze called and told me the following story which appeared in an article I wrote for the *Kountze News* under the headline, "'It seemed like a huge, hairy ape-like creature,' said a Fink."

"What's seven feet tall, has a dark, shaggy coat, massive short legs and long arms and looks like a huge hairy ape? That's what Sharon Gossett, formerly Sharon Votaw, of Kountze and the Rat Finks have been asking themselves since they saw the whatever-it-was in 1965. The Rat Finks was an informal club of Kountze High School kids who used to amuse themselves by going 'booger hunting.'

"The purpose of such hunting was not actually to find anything so much as to scare the living daylights out of new, uninitiated members of the club. The Rat Finks made frequent trips to places like Bragg Road and apparently became so accustomed to the Bragg Light as to virtually lose their fear of it. On a visit to one of their other favorite booger hunting grounds, however, the Rat Finks got a little more than they bargained for. They apparently found a real 'booger.'

"There is a monument in the cemetery at Old Hardin that is mounted by a statue of an angel pointing to the heavens. The Rat Finks called it the talking angel and would take their new members to the cemetery to ask it questions. The legend was, they said, that if upon calling upon the angel it did not answer you, you were doomed. Something tells me they would have felt considerably more doomed if it had talked, but you can imagine how the creepy surroundings of a cemetery and the ghost story prompting of the Rat Finks would have affected the nerves and imaginations of those unfortunate new initiates.

"On one such occasion their arcane ceremony was disrupted by a shadowy form running across the cemetery. It ran into a shed on the cemetery grounds, turning over cans and maintenance equipment, and making a noisy ruckus. Obviously, under the circumstances they had created, those kids did not take the time to investigate the disturbance; they got the blazes out of there as fast as they could. But before they could leave, they all got a look at the 'thing,' and in their horror they could scarcely believe their eyes. It seemed to be a huge, hairy ape-like creature. Of course, the cool, detached analyst of such situations, who is invariably someone who was not an eyewitness, would say that the fear and imaginations of the kids had caused them to see more than was actually there. Perhaps the Rat Finks knew that if they ever told anyone about their experience they would get that criticism, or perhaps they were just plain foolhardy, but in any case they persuaded an aunt of one of the girls to return with them to the cemetery for another look and to verify their sighting.

"Not only did they see the creature again, and not only did they all agree again on the general description of it, but this time it followed them as they made their hasty retreat after having seen it. It loped alongside the car in a manner again reminiscent of an ape. You would think that would have been enough for one night for the Rat Finks, but not so. They left the horrified aunt at her house and found themselves a male volunteer to take along with them for yet another look at the thing, thinking that this would provide them with some protection. Well, they saw it all right, and their "protection" passed out on the spot.

"By now you're probably asking yourself why you should believe this tale. Unless you see something like this for yourself it may be hard for you to imagine how anyone could seriously entertain the notion that such huge, hairy ape-like creatures could actually exist, but before you summarily dismiss this story as the wild imaginings of a few high school kids, you should consider that similar sightings are recorded the world over. In California and the Pacific Northwest in the Sierra and Cascade mountain range there have been repeated sightings of what they call the Bigfoot. In the Big Cypress Swamp in Florida, trappers have reported seeing what they called a skunk ape. Six years ago a movie was made on a similar creature that is supposed to have appeared in the bottom land swamps of Arkansas near the Louisiana border. In every case the creature described was very similar to that reported by the Rat Finks. It is also interesting to note that the grandmother of one of the Rat Finks told the girls that she could remember hearing of similar sightings near Old Hardin in the Cypress Creek bottoms from when she was a child.

"Perhaps others of our readers have experienced such unusual sightings. We would appreciate your sharing them with us as Sharon has done. You should not be afraid of having others think that you are strange or weird; Sharon and I won't. We and others know that it is not we who are strange; it is this wonderful and mysterious place known as the Big Thicket that is strange. So strange, in fact, as to convince me that the boundary between our everyday world and that of the Unknown, which we take to be so rigid, is at best tenuous and subject to being crossed—from either side."

Other responses from this article were even more bizarre than the Rat Fink story, and I quite frankly put this line of inquiry on hold for some time because I was having a hard time believing what I was being told. The most remarkable of these accounts involved both a big hairy creature and Bragg Road, a fact which, had I not known about Persinger's work, would have made me suspicious that the story was fabricated.

A young couple had innocently gone to look for the ghost light, naively assuming there was no risk to such an adventure, when something large and hairy suddenly pounced on their hood and glared menacingly at them through the windshield. The couple was naturally terrified. Luckily, the gentleman involved just happened to have his shotgun on a rack in the pickup and without hesitation pulled it down and emptied both barrels at the beast through the plate glass. The lady who called the story in said the couple was so badly shaken by the incident that they had confided only in her and a few other friends and would not speak to me about it for fear of being ridiculed by those who would not believe them. She assured me, however, that she had seen the holes in the windshield, and that there was another piece of compelling evidence that made her believe her friends' story. There were two sets of claw marks scratched deeply into the paint surface of the pickup's hood, which the creature left before it dismounted and ran screaming into the woods.

There was another person who also claimed to have had an encounter with a big, hairy man or ape-like creature on Bragg Road, but her story was even more fantastic. She claimed that a carload of horrified and astonished witnesses would back up her story that the light they saw on Bragg Road actually seemed to assume the form of a man. These last two stories were too much for me to deal with at the time. Either these people were amusing themselves at my expense or the wild man was considerably weirder than I had imagined. As unbelievable as these stories were, there was something compelling about the witnesses that kept me from totally dismissing their accounts. The association of the light with the wild man, far from discrediting these stories, fantastic as they are, was consistent with, and maybe even corroborated, Persinger and LaFreniere's observations. Almost ten years after collecting the stories at the Kountze News, circumstances again allowed me to remain in Southeast Texas long enough to renew my research on the Big Thicket Wild Man. I was by then thoroughly convinced that the Hardin County sightings were legitimate and that they constituted a genuine mystery. I was beginning to see how the Big Thicket sightings fit into a much larger pattern and I also had some idea of a methodology to pursue in gathering more information.

If the sightings were not merely spurious curiosities, more of them must have occurred since my readers had shared their stories with me. Unlike when I was with the newspaper in Kountze, there was no easy access to a large and random number of individuals who were likely to have spent large amounts of time in the woods and who would thus be likely to constitute a significant pool of potential witnesses. With this in mind, and at the suggestion of a friend, I contacted the president of the Big Thicket Association (BTA) in Saratoga.

The BTA operated a museum in Saratoga that had a steady stream of visitors from throughout the region. The association also had a substantial membership in rural areas in Hardin and adjoining counties, and had served as a clearinghouse for information on the Thicket ever since its instrumental role in helping to get legislation passed to create the Big Thicket National Preserve. This seemed a likely and logical place to look for witnesses, but it wasn't totally a rational process that led me to begin there. It was also a hunch.

Experience had taught me that somehow the mysterious power of "coincidences" can sometimes play a major role in this general kind of research. When I had discussed contacting the Big Thicket Association with a friend in Sour Lake who was interested in the research, she mentioned that she knew the president of the BTA personally and that they had had a recent conversation about Whitley Streiber's then current book, *Communion,* which they had both recently read

Coincidentally, I had also just read that book and had even corresponded with Streiber and considered some of his conclusions on UFOs and alien abductions to be relevant to my own studies of strange phenomena in the Big Thicket region.

Admittedly, Streiber's book had been a bestseller only a couple of years earlier, and it wouldn't be too much of a stretch to find someone even in rural Hardin County that would have an interest in reading it, but somehow the knowledge that the president of the BTA was open to the possibility of beings from other worlds interacting with humans reassured me that she wouldn't think it too weird if I asked her about wild man sightings in the area.

When I called her I again tried to avoid making any direct reference to the previous sightings or to anything else that would affect her response. All I asked was if she knew of any reports of unusual large animals that the association might have received within the last few years. Indeed, she said that quite recently a family from Saratoga had reported seeing what they called a large, hairy ape-like creature near the boundary of the Preserve.

No sooner had she said this than the phone rang on my office's other line. I put her on hold and answered. The voice on the other end asked to speak with Reba Riggs. I assumed, amidst considerable confusion, that someone had mistaken me for someone else, since my name, Rob Riggs, is the virtual male equivalent of the name of the person the caller was asking for. It turned out that the caller had misdialed the number he was trying to reach by one digit and ended up getting someone, who happened to be alone in the office at the time, with almost the same name of the person he intended to call. With strains of the "Twilight Zone" theme running through my head, I resumed the other conversation and chuckled under my breath at what seemed a reminder that I was dealing with something that doesn't operate totally within the laws of the world as it is normally understood.

The BTA lady said that she frankly had not paid much attention to the Saratoga family's report, which seemed a bit odd to me since there were apparently multiple witnesses. She said that the family who claimed to have seen the ape-like thing was of questionable reputation and no one had paid much attention to their report. Wanting to judge that for myself, I pressed her for any more details she could remember of their account.

She said they had seen the thing at dusk near an abandoned sludge pit in the old oil field near the boundary of the Preserve. They saw it clearly enough to see that it wasn't human. It was covered with long, shaggy hair and was much larger than a man. But the thing that convinced them that it wasn't human was its howl. When the creature became aware of their presence, it turned and scowled at them and ran howling into the cover of the darkening woods. It was unimaginable, they said, that anything merely human could produce such a howl. I was unable to interview the family myself since they had no telephone and adequate directions to their home, which was on the edge of the woods and well off the nearest paved road, were not available. Before long, however, corroboration of their sighting would come from an entirely independent source.

Just a few weeks after my conversation with its president, the BTA held its annual Halloween spook house for the area kids at its facility next to the museum. I thought this would be a great opportunity to talk to a lot of people, a high percentage of whom might have seen something unusual in the local woods. At the suggestion of Jeanie Turk, a friend from Pinewood, we went to the spook house equipped with a tape recorder, a card table and a few folding chairs. We set up near the entrance and attempted to engage the revelers in conversation.

The infamous Ghost Road was only a few miles away, and an organized walk down its spooky eight-mile sandy length was being offered to those brave enough to risk it as the ultimate celebration of Halloween. It was a simple matter to get people to talk about what they had seen or had not seen and to reminisce about any other excursions they may have made to the Ghost Road.

Rural Hardin County is hard-core provincial, though, and the locals are suspicious of outsiders. Speaking with the best elements of what was left of my East Texas accent I made sure that the group that had begun to gather knew that I was from Sour Lake, that my mother was born in Saratoga and that my great grandfather was buried in the Saratoga cemetery with the only Confederate Veteran's tombstone in the graveyard. This put the locals more at ease with me. The festive Halloween atmosphere seemed to make everyone feel a bit impish, and in no time at all a lively conversation ensued with participants dropping in and out as they made their way to and from the spook house entrance.

I soon heard the kind of information I expected to get. A lady from nearby Batson told of "Ol' Mossyback," which is apparently the local name for their version of the wild man. For years people in the area between the Thicket's western edge along the Pine Island Bayou and the Trinity River swamp had occasionally caught glimpses of something large, hairy and not quite human. The thing was usually seen as it was running away after the startled shrieks and howls of terrified livestock and dogs gave away its presence. On some of these occasions, the lady claimed, the creature was said to have left large footprints. Just recently, in fact, a friend of hers had seen such a set of prints in the sand alongside a country road in the area.

Another lady from Saratoga said she didn't know if it was what we were talking about, but one night not long before our conversation something huge and menacing had chased her son and some of his hunting buddies out of the nearby Garcia Woods. They managed to make it to their pickup before it could catch them, but they heard a loud thump and felt the truck shake as they made their hasty retreat. The thing had apparently kicked the rear bumper and left a considerable dent in it.

Three teen-age boys on the periphery of the group that had

gathered were listening intently to these stories. One of them, who identified himself only as Buckshot, stepped forward and told me that they had all seen an "ape-looking critter" in the nearby woods at least three different times.

There's not a whole lot for kids to do in Saratoga, which is little more than a wide clearing in the woods along the highway. Before the boys were old enough to have their driver's licenses and be able to drive the forty-odd miles to Beaumont for entertainment, they had come to make a hobby of taking extended hiking and camping trips into the Big Thicket National Preserve on weekends. The Preserve is adjacent to the city limits of Saratoga, and the boys spent many pleasant and adventurous hours exploring the deep woods which literally came up to their back doors.

From this pastime they proudly called themselves the "Thicketeers," a name reflective of their rural East Texas roots which still respect woodsmanship. With Buckshot continuing as their spokesman, but with all three pitching in, the boys began to relate their sightings. In their naiveté they did not seem to fully realize the remarkable nature of what they had seen.

I found their unaffected country ways refreshing, but something about their almost matter-of-fact attitude made me suspicious. It did not seem to strike them as particularly strange that an "ape-like critter" apparently inhabits the local woods. True, they probably grew up, as I had, with the attitude that there could be anything in the form of man or beast in the Thicket, but I began to wonder whether they were putting me on. Despite their apparent innocence, they might have heard or read about the creature they were describing from some other source and were good-naturedly amusing themselves at the expense of a stranger they were not likely to ever see again.

I asked Buckshot if he had ever read anything about Sasquatch. He was unfamiliar with the term, so I asked him if he had ever heard of Bigfoot. This was vaguely familiar to him, but before he could answer, one of the other boys caught my drift and spoke up. "Mister, I can tell you Buckshot didn't read about this in no book."

"How is that?" I replied.

" 'Cause Buckshot don't read no books."

Having established at least this much, it seemed that a good way to test the veracity of their claims might be to compare the details of their sightings with those of the Saratoga family I had heard about from the Big Thicket Association president.

"Do y'all know the Smith [as I shall call them] family?" I asked. They all nodded in the affirmative. "Well, I'm told they also claim to have seen an ape-like critter in the woods somewhere around here." Buckshot thought that was interesting but that they were probably lying. The whole town knew they were not to be trusted, and hardly anyone spoke to them much or socialized with them. We dropped the matter and they continued with more details of their sighting.

The boys related that they had seen the ape on three occasions. The first time was from a distance of several hundred yards across a rice field as the three were riding in the back of a pickup between Saratoga and Sour Lake. The creature was running on all fours. Just as they realized it was something unusual, it disappeared into the woods that border the field. Another time, during one of their Thicketeer expeditions, they saw it from much closer up near an abandoned bridge that crosses a bayou near the boundary of the Big Thicket Preserve. But their most remarkable sighting, they said, occurred in the same area as the bridge near a sludge pit that had been part of an old oil field before the establishment of the Preserve. This latest bit of information began to sound familiar.

"What time of day was it when you all saw the ape by the

sludge pit?" I asked, playing a strong hunch. They all agreed that it was right at dusk. Even in the lengthening shadows cast by the nearby forest's edge they could see that it was similar, if not identical, to the ape they had seen earlier at the abandoned bridge. "If you all saw it at dusk by a sludge pit in the area you have described, then you probably heard it howl," I guessed, confident what their response would be.

"How did you know that?" Buckshot said, looking as if his mind had just been read.

"The Smiths said they saw it at dusk by a sludge pit in what sounds like the same area you all saw it. They said it howled at them just before it disappeared into the shadows." There followed a brief moment of silence, as if all three boys were surprised at this news.

"Well, I'll be," Buckshot drawled, "maybe they weren't lying after all."

The Thicketeers offered to take me to the old bridge where they thought the ape lived, a conclusion that makes you wonder about the Scandinavian legends of Trolls living under bridges in remote places. The boys seemed to have told their tales with complete candor and their offer to assist in further research of the Hardin County wild man mystery seemed sincere. They gave me their phone numbers, but I hesitated to involve those kids any further in the research.

They were obviously puzzled at my suggestion that we would go unarmed if we were to go looking for the wild man. The thought of their brandishing their deer rifles, even in self-defense, didn't set right with me. The Thicketeers had grown up in a hunting tradition, and their trigger fingers might be a little bit itchy. The temptation of the notoriety that would come from bagging a truly exceptional trophy might be too hard to resist, and the idea of killing the beast as if collecting a specimen to prove its existence was not appealing. I also didn't want to be responsible for the safety of those kids, because there was no telling what the wild man's capabilities might be.

In any case, the Saratoga spook house interviews were quite productive. The Smith family's story was corroborated by that of the Thicketeers, and both stories taken together with those collected earlier seemed to suggest patterns in the wild man's behavior and range.

The creature was usually seen either at night or at dusk; the one daylight sighting that the Thicketeers had from the back of a pickup was the sole exception. The creature is ape-like and generally bipedal, but it is also known to go about on all fours. At least two separate parties of multiple witnesses heard it howl with a volume they felt was humanly impossible. The creature was usually seen in the immediate vicinity of a body of water—either a sludge pit, creek or bayou. Of course, the thickest and most inaccessible parts of the Big Thicket woods are the creek bottoms, so it should come as no surprise that the ape would seek shelter and cover there. It also began to appear that particular streams may constitute part of its range. The Smith and Thicketeer sightings were all either directly beside or within a short distance of the Little Pine Island Bayou. Is it mere coincidence that virtually the entire length of this stream is within a federally protected preserve, where hunting and even bearing loaded firearms is largely prohibited?

Not long after the spook house interviews I obtained accounts of more sightings on that same bayou some twenty to thirty miles downstream of Saratoga. Between Sour Lake and Beaumont is a favorite parking spot for teen-agers. It is secluded by dense bottomland woods, which extend to the Little Pine Island Bayou, no more than a hundred yards or so away. Several carloads of startled teens have been terrorized there by what has become known as the "Raggedy Man." Witnesses have consistently reported that the Raggedy Man came right up to the car windshields and peered in curiously.

It is described as being much taller and of heavier build than an average man. Its long hair, scraggly beard, and not-quite-human expression gave rise to its name. No one has reported that the Raggedy Man was naked, but it's not clear that anyone ever hung around long enough after its appearances to notice one way or another. It is likely, though, that the Raggedy Man stories are further instances of the ape-man/wild man sightings from further upstream.

Mike, who did not wish to be further identified, lives in a nearby subdivision that is bisected by the Little Pine Island Bayou, and is adjacent to thick woods, may also have had an encounter with the creature. Late one night he happened to be walking home when he heard something growling at him menacingly from the nearby edge of the woods. His gut reaction was to run for it. He looked back to see what he thought was a huge, dark dog chasing him. The thing got close enough for Mike to hear, not only its growling, but also its nails clicking on the pavement of the road.

Suddenly a car appeared behind Mike and stopped and turned around after it passed him. The "dog" apparently retreated back into the woods. The driver offered Mike a ride home. Mike thanked him for stopping and for saving him from the dog.

"What dog?" the driver asked.

"The dog that was chasing me," Mike repeated.

"That was no dog that was chasing you," the driver answered. He didn't get a real good look at it, but whatever was chasing Mike was running upright, like a man.

I have already noted that creatures similar in description to the Big Thicket wild man have been reported from various other parts of the country, and that it is part of an enigma of vast proportions. Furthermore, there are certain patterns of appearance and behavior that legitimize the Hardin County sightings by showing that there is an objectivity of information obtained from having witnesses unknown to one another. The Hardin County sightings are also legitimized by the fact that the patterns observed in them are consistent with the details of sightings obtained by other researchers of big, hairy monsters, or ape-like creatures in other parts of the country.

To put all of this in perspective and see how the Big Thicket may offer unique opportunities for the study of this phenomenon and its profound significance to our knowledge of the world, I will begin by referring again to the work of Persinger and Lafreniere. They claim that "A variety of primates exists over the surface of the earth. Most non-human primates live primarily in rain forests or in tropical areas. These have been classified and are established branches of the zoological tree. However, there are other reports of primate-like creatures which exist throughout the world. Such creatures have not been classified, nor have they been systematically studied. They exist as transient phenomena." What they mean by transient phenomena will become more apparent later, but further on in their discussion of mystery primate sightings they note that, "high pitched screams have also been associated with humanoid observations."

The screams or howls of the hairy wild man are further noted by a number of other researchers. In the book *In Search of the Spirit of Place,* James Swan writes that a typical sighting is often accompanied by "a high-pitched whining scream that is ear-splitting." B. Ann Slate and Alan Berry describe it variously from the reports of a number of witnesses.

"It was awful—the most frightening sound I've ever heard from that close up."

"I've never heard a sound like that in all my years in the woods."

"It began as a growl, only it drew out, building into a loud, vibrating crescendo. It was like a gorilla's display, one can imagine, only the voice was louder than any man's or animal's Alan had ever heard, short of an elephant or perhaps a tiger."

This last description is reminiscent of the account from the Hardin County man who heard the howl but did not actually see the wild man in the darkness about an hour before dawn. He was close enough so that he said that it made his ears ring and, "the very air seemed to vibrate."

John Green, author of *Sasquatch: The Apes Among Us,* describes the cry of the ape-like creature as like "a man in pain yelling." John Keel, in his *The Complete Guide to Mysterious Beings,* reports that a "Booger" (this seems to be the preferred term in the South to refer to the creatures) seen near Clanton, Alabama, was described by witnesses as making a sound "like a woman screaming," and that "others said it sounded more like an elephant."

Virtually all researchers of large hairy humanoids cite footprints as compelling physical evidence for the objective existence of the creatures. In most cases the prints are about eighteen inches long and about eight-to-ten inches wide. Keel's description of Yeti tracks seen in the Himalayas is typical: "It was definitely not an ape or a bear, and the prints were much too big to have been made by a barefooted man."

Like its Bigfoot and Yeti counterparts, the Big Thicket wild man has reportedly left clear tracks on a number of occasions. We have already seen that the Hardin County Sheriff's Office investigated such tracks during the wild man sightings flap in the 1950s. The Saratoga spook house interviews yielded the Ol' Mossyback stories complete with accounts of its huge prints.

An expert Big Thicket guide of my acquaintance told me of several sets of unusually large barefoot prints he had once come across in the vicinity of Black Creek deep in the Rosier Unit of the Big Thicket Preserve and miles from the nearest paved road. He had thought they were a bit odd at the time but just assumed that they had been made by an extraordinarily big old boy. When I pointed out the problem with this assumption, he agreed that is was unlikely that any normal person, big or not, would be walking about barefoot in the Thicket, which has virtually every description of thorn, sticker and spiny vine, not to mention stinging insects and snakes.

We have noted that the wild man is frequently seen near a creek or bayou. This is typical of Bigfoot, ape-man type sightings throughout the country. In his *Mysterious America* researcher Loren Coleman notes that there are "a high percentage of sightings along the creek bottoms of rural America," and further comments that, "The documentary movie about Fouke, Arkansas's, ape-like 'monster,' *The Legend of Boggy Creek,* notes several times that 'he always travels the creeks.'" Keel also noted of the Clanton, Alabama, sightings that the creature "ranged up and down the creek for a distance of some ten miles."

Coleman observes that most of the sightings in the U.S. outside of the Pacific Northwest occur in the river bottoms of the Mississippi Valley and its tributaries. Of this area he notes that, "These Bottomlands, as they are technically termed, cover a good deal of the South and are more or less unexplored and ignored— most unfortunately, for hidden deep in the Bottomlands waits what could be the zoological discovery of the century." He goes on to postulate that there may be a remnant population of a native species of great ape, assumed to have long been extinct, that still inhabits the swamps and bottomlands of North America, particularly in the Deep South of the United States. Coleman's work in studying and documenting ape-man sightings is of inestimable value, however, if the conclusions we are headed toward are any indication, when the nature of these ape-man creatures is finally understood, it may constitute a discovery that is considerably more than a zoological breakthrough.

If there is a species of wild man or ape afoot in America, whatever its nature might be, we would expect a considerable history of sightings. Green writes that, "Research into old, long forgotten records has confirmed that reports of such creatures have been continual, from the original Indian inhabitants of North America and from the explorers and fur traders who invaded the unmapped interior." Coleman traces the recorded history of such sightings back to 1869 to the western edge of the great bottomlands network along the Osage River in Kansas. Residents of the area called it a wild man or gorilla. Coleman writes of the sightings that "...local opinion held that the thing was a gorilla or large orangutan which had escaped from some menagerie."

There is an amusing parallel to this in the case of the Big Thicket ape-man. The late Lance Rosier was a Big Thicket guide and self-taught naturalist of considerable renown. It seems that one day someone found the remains of what was described as a baboon alongside a Hardin County highway. The story goes that a passing one-ring circus had a fatality in its meager menagerie and had simply dumped the remains. Whether this was known for a fact or was merely assumed is an interesting point for speculation in the light of what we have seen, but in any case it was taken to Lance for identification. Pete Gunter, who wrote of the incident in his *Big Thicket: A Challenge for Conservation,* reported Lance's reply, "from the look on its face, and its stooped neck, and the calluses on the seat of its britches, I'd say it's a retired East Texas domino player."

Even if Lance had shared the suspicions of those who

brought him the ape, there are interesting circumstances that cloud the issue of whether it was a mere recent escapee. Feral apes and monkeys have, indeed, been known to thrive in the Big Thicket environment. Coleman, in his discussion of the possibility of an undiscovered species of great ape in the bottomlands of North America, noted that a colony of baboons had been sighted along the Trinity River, which is the western edge of the Thicket country.

Dempsie Henley's *The Big Thicket Story* notes that on the outdoors page of the November 26, 1966, edition of the *Beaumont Enterprise,* right next to an account of four men killing a 400 pound black bear near Pineland in East Texas, there was a story complete with pictures about two Beaumont men who shot what was apparently an escapee monkey. Mike Webster and W. T. Holland were hunting in the Big Thicket between Woodville and Silsbee. They had already taken about five squirrels when they saw what they thought were a couple of fox squirrels in a tall white oak tree. They both fired and when they went to pick up the fallen squirrel they were surprised to find that it wasn't a squirrel they had bagged, but a monkey.

The monkey was reddish-brown, similar in color to a fox squirrel, and about the size of a big house cat. The men said they saw another monkey in the tree after they realized what they had shot. It was perched near what appeared to be a nest made of moss. This led the article's author, Jim Arledge, to speculate that there might have been an established colony of the monkeys and that it wasn't just a single escapee.

Could a feral baboon population, then, be the origin of the "Ol' Mossyback" legend of the Trinity River swamp? Coleman thinks it unlikely that either feral or escapee apes could account for the ape-like creature sightings of the American bottomlands. He points out that primate escapees are too rare to account for the number of sightings, and that the behavior of the creatures that are sighted is not consistent with that of the species that are allegedly feral or escapees. Coleman concludes that,"…a rather free-ranging, swimming, nocturnal ape already exists in many parts of the southern United States."

A story I heard from a group of young men from Dayton one night on Bragg Road supports Coleman's conclusion and is likely evidence that the "Old Mossyback" sightings cannot be account-ed for by feral baboons. John (whose last name is withheld to pro-tect his privacy), a friend of theirs, used to join them in such adventures as outings to Bragg Road and on overnight camping and hunting trips in the woods. But John no longer participates in any of these night-time activities in the woods, because he had an encounter with something that apparently traumatized him.

John's family home is on the edge of the Trinity River swamps near Dayton. One night he heard a disturbance on the porch where he kept a pen of rabbits. He investigated just in time to see a large, dark form make off with rabbit in hand. John impulsively followed in hot pursuit, staying close enough to hear the rabbit squeal continuously, not really knowing what he was chasing or what he would do if he caught it. It was a short dis-tance through thick woods to the bank of the river. Standing on the high bank in the moonlight he watched dumb-struck as what looked like a huge ape-like animal swam to the other side of the river, easily negotiating the strong current, and never letting go of the rabbit.

Since this experience, which was witnessed by a friend who had been at John's home that night, John will not spend the night in the woods–not alone, not with his group of buddies, not with all of them armed to the teeth. He has no desire to risk con-fronting the beast in its own element under the cover of darkness. The boys told us that there had been other sightings of the creature in the area and that it had come to be called the "Route Monster."

This story seems to support Coleman's notion of a nocturnal, swimming ape, and it is consistent with most of the sightings mentioned here. The wild man is virtually always seen at night or at dusk. Although the Route Monster is the only instance I know of in which the creature was seen actually swimming, it is, as we have already mentioned, usually seen near a stream or body of water. Coleman's other contention that the ape is wide-ranging is also confirmed by the distribution of sightings over a considerable area in Hardin, Liberty, Jefferson, Polk, and Tyler counties in the Southeast Texas Big Thicket country.

Other researchers have recorded particulars of ape-man sightings that parallel in some details the Hardin County sightings. Keel, for example, reports that a creature seen outside Knoxville, Tennessee, in 1959 left, "two long scratches on the hood," of the car. In another incident, which took place in 1969 at Lake Worth, Texas, outside Fort Worth, witnesses told police that a 7-foot hairy creature, "had pounced on their car and left scratch marks on the hood." In yet another case near Elfers, Florida, Keel reports that witnesses claimed that, "an animal about the size of a large chimpanzee sprang onto the hood of the car." With such reports gathered by other researchers the account I was given while at the *Kountze News* seems less fantastic. One only wonders if any of the witnesses in the Knoxville, Lake Worth and Florida incidences happened to have their shotguns with them like the couple on Bragg Road.

Keel also writes of a hairy monster seen near Fontana, California, that is described by witnesses, "as being seven-feet tall, with brown hair and covered with moss and slime." It seems likely that the Ol' Mossyback stories in the Trinity swamp emerged from sightings of something very similar. There is also an intriguing parallel to the wild man seen by a sludge pit on several occasions. It seems that its counterpart in the Pacific Northwest has a similar affinity for gravel pits. Don Hunter and René Dahinden, writing of a man-animal seen near Richland, Washington, in 1966, state that it is, "seen frequently in the area of some old gravel pits outside the town." Slate and Berry in describing another creature sighting in the Northwest write of the witness that, "He said that he had just seen a man who stood between nine and ten feet tall in the road by a gravel pit where he'd been cutting wood."

The one thing that sludge pits and gravel pits have in common is that they are penetrations of the earth's surface. Of a Bigfoot sighting area in Oregon, researchers Hunter and Dahinden note that, "The area outside the Dalles where this happened is studded with old mines and natural caves and the youths believed this was where the creatures concealed themselves in daylight."

Other researchers have consistently noted that hairy humanoid creature sightings are common around abandoned mine shafts and quarries. As we shall see later, these openings in the earth, rather than being a means of concealment, may have more to do with where the creatures come from.

Another common feature reported of the creatures is their uncommonly bad odor. In the Big Cypress Swamp in Florida there are legends of what is called the Skunk Ape. Keel summarizes these descriptions and reports that witnesses described the stench of the monsters variously as "moldy, rancid, like stale urine, like something rotten." Although I have never had this specifically reported of the Big Thicket wild man, on one expedition into the Thicket our party encountered the tell-tale stench in an area where one of the group had heard the familiar howling sound not long before. It smelled exactly like a very ripe putrefying carcass. The odor covered a considerable area, and after searching the area where the smell lingered, we found no sign of carrion.

If Coleman is correct and these ape creatures have established populations in the Deep South, then we would expect an established tradition of sightings. Green's research indicates this is exactly the case, and he reports that "The 'Woolybooger' also crops up in print from time to time and it seems to me to indicate quite definitely that there is a widely distributed tradition of hairy bipeds in the South." No doubt, our "booger" hunting Rat Fink friends from Kountze would not dispute this point.

If the Big Thicket sightings are not spurious or suspiciously isolated instances, then we would expect a tradition of sightings throughout East Texas, since it is the southern and western extent of the Southern bottomlands and swamps that seem to be the creature's preferred habitat. Green notes that there are numerous reports from northeast Texas, particularly in the extreme northeast corner near the Arkansas border. Sightings near Haskell, Texas, he says, have been so numerous for at least the past 80 years, that the locals have taken to calling it the "Haskell Rascal." Haskell is just across the state line from Fouke, Arkansas, scene of *The Legend of Boggy Creek.*

In Stephens County, Texas, Green reports sightings of "an ape-shaped animal that became known as the 'critter' –described by a rancher who shot at it as being seven feet tall and four feet wide and covered with hair." Although sightings in other parts of Texas and the Southwest are rare, Green notes that there have been isolated sightings of ape-like creatures in Texas near Denton, Corsicana, San Antonio, and Lake Travis in the Texas Hill Country.

We could add that there was a spate of sightings a few years back along the Little River near Cameron in Central Texas, and that there is a road near Round Rock in the Austin area named Hairy Man Road, for sightings that occurred in that area near a creek bottom. Unfortunately, there are not likely to be many more sightings near Round Rock or Lake Travis due to the explosive growth in the Hill Country region near Austin in the last twenty years. About the only wild men you could expect to encounter in that part of Texas these days would be money-crazed real estate developers.

Thanks in part to the creation twenty years ago of a national preserve, the Big Thicket region is the one part of Texas that still has vast stretches of bottomlands habitat. The Thicket appears to be the most active part of Texas for large, unknown, hairy primate, ape-man, or wild man-type sightings. Aside from a few isolated pockets in the northeastern part of the state, the Thicket country appears to be the only part of Texas, and certainly the largest general region, with a sustained history of sightings sufficient for the mysterious creature to have been incorporated into the region's folklore.

If the Thicket were to be included in an even broader region with traditions of such sightings, such as the Pacific Northwest Bigfoot country of California, Oregon and Washington, we would need to look, not elsewhere in Texas, and not even elsewhere in the Pineywoods of East Texas, but rather to the adjacent Bayou Country of South Louisiana.

In many ways the Big Thicket is little more than the western extent of the Bayou Country. In fact, in terms of climate, terrain and vegetation, and strong Cajun and Creole cultural influence, Southeast Texas from east of the Trinity swamps to the Sabine River is a first cousin to South Louisiana and a distant relative of most of the rest of Texas. Like the Big Thicket, the Bayou Country was isolated from the rest of the world for years by thick woods and deep swamps. The Cajuns and Creoles, (French speaking Blacks), especially on the Louisiana side of the Sabine, were further isolated by their language well up until after World War II when the oil boom that had led to the populating of the Big Thicket region in Texas came to their marshes and bayous and brought increased cultural contact with the outside world.

As might be expected then, South Louisiana has a rich tradition and history of encounters with wild man-type creatures. Typical examples are detailed in John Bergeron's anthology, *Bayou Cajuns: True Stories from the Louisiana Bayou People.* Leroy Coates, in an entry entitled "Bigfoot Roams the Woods Near Columbia," describes a sighting that took place on the Coates farm near Columbia, Louisiana.

Mr. and Mrs. Coates were working late one evening just past sundown on their farm in a 40 acre pasture that is surrounded by woods. In the quiet of the gathering dusk they heard a noise nearby. "Soon a dark, upright form broke out of the woods and raced across the pasture in the moonlight, moaning and growling as it ran. The couple was badly frightened by the sighting. Some days later Mr. Coates was awakened in the night by the frightened bawling of a calf from that same pasture only to find out the next morning that a 300 pound calf was missing from the herd with no signs as to what might have caused its disappearance."

Mrs. Coates saw the creature again a few days later while driving home one afternoon. "A large, hairy creature about 7 ft. tall dashed across the road in front of her car, and ran into the woods next to the road, and stood behind a small bush. Mrs. Coates stopped and rolled her window down to get a better look and described the creature as having human-like features and being covered with shaggy hair–even on its face."

Perhaps in part due to their years of cultural and geographical isolation, Bayou Country people have incorporated the quality of strangeness of the hairy humanoid creatures and the circumstances of their sightings into their folklore, and not merely the fact of the sightings. It is relatively easy to believe that there might be some rare and unknown form of ape or even a primitive form of man that coexists with us in isolated wilderness areas of the world. But there are circumstances that surround the wild man and ape sightings, give the creatures an aura of intense strangeness, and remove them from the status of zoological or anthropological oddities to that of genuine mysteries.

I first encountered this quality of strangeness in the association of the wild man with the light seen on Bragg Road, particularly in the unbelievable story already cited of a carload of witnesses that felt like the wild man had materialized from the light. We have already seen that the creatures are frequently seen in the vicinity of pits, creeks and large bodies of water. It is perhaps the combination of the association with water, penetrations of the earth, and mysterious energy manifestations that has led the Bayou people to traditionally associate the hairy humanoids with what we would today consider superstitious beliefs.

Sidney Concianne, in an entry entitled "Roogaroos on the Bayous Near Dulac" in Bergeron's anthology, describes the legend of the Sabine Indians concerning a fierce, hairy human-like creature that is said to sometimes come up from the depths of the dark bayou waters to attack unsuspecting shrimpers and fishermen. Such attacks are usually associated with the victims' having broken some taboo, such as dropping their nets into the wrong part of the bayou. Such an act, rather than arbitrarily being considered taboo, might amount to the fishermen's not having acknowledged the creature's existence or not having respected its domain. As the instances of claw marks left on attacked vehicles will attest, this may be more than mere superstition. Does the wild man of Hardin County have a territorial protective instinct that it sometimes considers violated by those who happen to be at just the wrong place at just the wrong time on Bragg Road or elsewhere in their domain?

Could the swimming apes that Coleman postulates and the Route Monster of the Trinity bottoms be related to the Cajun legends? Is roogaroo just another name for Bigfoot or wild man? Concianne also mentions that stories of "roogaroos" come from all over Cajun country. "The only difference," he says, "is that the highland Cajuns call them "Loup Garoux" or "Werewolf." Similarly, isolated sightings in the Thicket have come to refer to the "Dog Man." This may refer to the creature's running on all fours at times, and its howling and growling.

Just in terms of appearance, it is understandable how a large, hairy, human-like creature could come to be called a werewolf. The term also has another association, though, that of shape-shifting or changing from one form to another. We usually think of werewolves as changing from a normal human form to that of a man/animal. Could loup garoux legends be associated with hairy wild men having changed from energy or light-forms? Our photograph with the wild man's face in the luminous fog, the stories of the wild man's emerging from the light on Bragg Road, and Devereux's accounts of human-like forms contained within vaporous lights, may well be related to the basis of the bayou loup garoux legends.

If there is a real connection between the wild man sightings and the mystery lights such as the Bragg Light, we would expect stories and legends of similar lights in the same region of South Louisiana where the loup garoux and roogaroo stories circulate. Actually, I learned of the existence of just such lights in Louisiana before learning that the wild man stories are duplicated there as well.

A group of college kids from the University of Southwestern Louisiana in Lafayette, (now the University of Louisiana-

Lafayette), who were working on a Cajun folklore project, visited with me while I was at the *Kountze News*. The fame of the Bragg Light had reached there and these kids realized that a mystery light that recurs near Gonzales, Louisiana, corresponded in detail with regards to size, appearance and behavior with what they had heard about its East Texas counterpart. The Gonzales light is recognized by both Coleman and Persinger as one of thirty-odd locations in North America with genuine recurring ghost lights. Incidentally, like Bragg, Marfa, and other ghost light locations we have cited, its location also falls near the 30th degree north latitude.

As in Texas, there is more than one place where such lights occur in South Louisiana. The Cajuns call them fifolet, according to J.J. Reneaux in his *Cajun Folktales,* which is slang for feu foulais or "compressed fire." Specific stories of the Big Thicket wild man lend support to what at first would be dismissed as superstitions of the roogaroo. If there is any basis to what Reneaux writes of the fifolet, the strangeness of the wild man in particular its having been seen by at least one party merging from the light on Bragg Road, and the Cajun association of the creatures with werewolves, may all be hints of a looming mystery of astonishing proportions.

In the land of voodoo and Marie Laveaux, the fifolet, like the roogaroo, is associated with magic and the psychic realm. Reneaux writes of an old man called Medeo who lived around the Atchafalaya swamp. Legend had it that he was a wizard possessed of evil powers, not the least of which was the ability to transform himself into a light-form. "Then, by the power of his evil spell, the wizard would change himself into a fifolet, a burning, shining ball of blue and white flames. He'd float out to the swamp, dancing and bobbing through the darkness, tempting all to follow him to destruction and death."

We have seen that the wild man stories of the Big Thicket may corroborate the roogaroo legends. We have also seen that the ghost lights and the energy that produces them are associated with the wild man sightings. From the testimony of eyewitnesses on Bragg Road, Devereux's stories of human-like forms emerging from luminous mists, and the evidence of the photograph taken on Bragg Road of a wild man's face emerging from the luminous "fog," it appears that the Medeo legend may have a basis in something other than fantasy. If balls of light can change into humanoid forms, perhaps the process can be reversed.

The association of mysterious light-form producing energies and ape-like creature sightings is reported again and again by independent researchers like Persinger, Keel, Devereux, and Coleman from remote places all over the world. The exact nature of the relation between the energy/light-forms and the sighted creatures remains a mystery, but this statement by Janet and Colin Bord reflects a consensus opinion among the most prominent researchers of the phenomenon: "That some alien animals are linked with electrical effects is indicated by an incident in the Monongahela National Forest, West Virginia, in October 1960 when a man driving his car saw an 8-foot hairy, ape-like 'monster with long hair standing straight up.' His car stopped and the driver had to sit and wait." Eventually the witness resumed his trip only to have the car falter again, "And sure enough, there beside the road stood the monster again." The points were completely burned out on the man's car.

In a similar incident in Illinois reported by the Bords, "a man's car came to a stop and as he got out a black cat-like animal emerged from the shadows, almost as if it had deliberately caused the car's engine to fail." This illustrates that it is not always ape-like creatures that are seen in these incidents, and this is particularly significant in the history of strange creature sightings in the

Big Thicket. We have dealt thus far with the ape/wild man category of mystery creatures that are frequently linked to the same areas where there are long standing recurrent ghost light manifestations. These are not the only mystery creatures reported in locations where periodic fluctuations in the local magnetic field apparently produce the ghost lights.

In their *Space Time Transients and Unusual Events,* Persinger and LaFreniere note that "One of the largest categories of infrequent and unusual events is concerned with the sudden increase in observations of large unknown animals." Along with what they term "unknown humanoids or primates," they list a category of "feline-like creatures." These are typically described as, "large, cat-like animals, typically yellowish or black," and their size is compared to that of large pumas or lions. Significantly, also associated with these creatures are reports of, "sounds of screeching or roaring."

Tales of screaming black "panthers" are even more common than those of the howling wild man in the Big Thicket country. They are so common that, unlike the wild man stories which may be debated as hoaxes by the locals or otherwise explained away, it is generally taken for granted that the black panther is part of the natural wildlife. Archer Fullingim, a former *Kountze News* publisher, described the situation in Abernethey's *Tales from the Big Thicket:* "Nearly everybody in the Big Thicket fervently believes that panthers may be tawny in color every other place, but in the Big Thicket they are coal black with scarlet mouths and scarlet tongues, and with eyes that shine in the dark. They also believe that panthers scream like a woman, and you can find hundreds of people who have heard panthers scream, despite the fact that naturalists argue that there is no such thing as a black panther in these parts and that panthers never ever scream, especially like a fear-crazed woman."

What complicates the issue is that the cougar or mountain lion, traditionally referred to in the Deep South as a panther, is native to the Big Thicket, as it once was to virtually all of North America. There is an increasing number of sightings of these animals in the area. Some of the black panther reports may actually be sightings of individuals of a dark phase of this species, which is reportedly more common in some places in the deep swamps of the South than the generally more common tawny-colored phase.

This would not account for the persistent reports of screaming sounds, however. Attempts to dismiss the stories on that account are also ignorant of another factor in the black panther sightings that removes them from any confusion with puma or cougar sightings—the same association with mysterious energies and light-forms as that of the wild man. Persinger, as well as Keel, Coleman, and Bord, have all reported the existence of large, black cat-like animals in the same areas where the energy fluctuations occur.

The story of the black cat seen near the "failed transformer" in the 1985 Beaumont blackout comes to mind here, and I can't help but wonder if this association of black cats with unusual energies has anything to do with the basis of the superstition about turning back if a black cat crosses your path. There might have been a time when this association was more widely known, and there might have been good reason to be cautious if a certain kind of black cat crossed your path.

A pioneer in the field of paranormal phenomena and crypto-zoological investigation, the late Ted Holiday of England, devoted an entire chapter of his book, *The Goblin Universe,* to the appearance of what he called the "mystery Big Cats" in Great Britain. Like those in the Thicket, British cats are commonly described as black in appearance with glowing eyes. Big cats have been extinct in the wild in Britain for well over a century, and that's probably the last place anyone would expect to encounter one, so their appearances are even more remarkable and less likely to be of a naturally occurring animal than in the Thicket.

Though these creatures appear to be physically real and leave some evidence, particularly footprints, Holiday reports that a peculiar quality of these animals is that they have been observed to literally vanish. For this reason they are traditionally associated with the spirit world or psychic realm. The legend of the big cats in Britain goes back a long way. Holiday says, "Even a superficial study of religion in Britain shows that the mystery puma has always been with us, although it used to be called a 'panther'." He names a number of medieval churches of England that featured carvings of the mystery panthers, usually depicted as doing battle with a saint, and adds that they were regarded as demonic manifestations.

This suggests a suppression, common at the time in the Church, of pre-Christian Celtic shamanistic belief in which powerful wizards were said to have the power to assume the forms of animals, including that of a black panther. Elements of this tradition form the basis of much of the background of Deepak Chopra's novel, *The Return of Merlin,* in which one of Merlin's apprentices often shape-shifts into a black panther. This calls to mind the Cajun legends of the loup garoux and the wizard, Medeo, and there are even more striking parallels. There are voodoo legends in South Louisiana that speak of the Cat People, who can supposedly shift forms from human to large black felines.

In at least one case recorded by Holiday the appearance of a black panther at Bushylease, England, was preceded several times by the appearance of the typical spherical ghost light and the strong ammonia-like smell that is so frequently associated with the large, hairy humanoid sightings. As you might expect, this pattern is repeated by the screaming black panthers of the Big Thicket.

Archer Fullingim's claim about the widespread belief in black panthers in the Big Thicket is not an exaggeration. Virtually anyone you talk to in Kountze, Saratoga, or Honey Island, who has spent much time in the woods or is old enough or country enough at least to have not spent his entire leisure time life in front of a television, will either claim to have seen and/or heard a black panther himself or know someone who has. I would have to include myself in their numbers, because although I personally have not seen or heard a panther, my grandfather, several friends, and a number of people I have interviewed have. The details on these sightings are generally sketchy, compared to the wild man sightings we have discussed, but there are two well documented sightings that are both compelling and authoritative. Both are attributed to the same source–the incomparable Lance Rosier of Saratoga.

Rosier, who was honored for his life-long efforts to conserve the Big Thicket by having a unit of the Preserve named for him, was the consummate Big Thicket guide. Out of his sheer love of the Thicket he taught himself from books the Latin name of virtually every tree, vine, flowering plant, and shrub in those woods. Eventually his knowledge was respected and regularly sought out by university scientists who came to him to guide them to his secret places. He was held in the highest esteem by the scientific community and had an impeccable reputation for honesty and the accuracy of his observations. At least two of his observations, though, were not consistent with scientific assumptions and for the most part have been politely ignored.

Maxine Johnston, who knew Lance personally and was also instrumental in Big Thicket conservation efforts, attributes the following quote to Lance in her book, *Thicket Explorer:* "But don't ever believe a panther cannot scream, because they can, and I have heard them many times in the Big Thicket. I saw a black panther in the late 1950s south of Saratoga, in the region where there are many may haw trees, on a ridge. He was a beautiful beast."

Another Lance sighting reported by Johnston confirms the screaming black panther's place in the Big Thicket's menagerie of strange beasts. Just as significantly, it also confirms the black panther's relation to the strange energy spikes that knock out electrical systems in both ghost light and wild man encounters. Johnston writes, "He said that he and his brother had been hunting in the Big Thicket, and as they were near the highway, coming out on a little-traveled road, their car went dead." After awhile they were able to get the engine to start again. "When less than 100 yards down the road, Lance said his brother called to tell him he had company. He looked back to see a big male panther. As it came even with him, and less than ten yards away, it stopped and screamed with a savage sound that would unnerve just about anyone."

There are theories that are beginning to emerge from reputable researchers who realize that the relation between manifestations of mystery creatures and the light-producing energy fields may lie at the basis of a mystery of profound significance. Persinger's laboratory research suggests that the same energy fields that manifest as ghost lights can affect the areas of the brain that organize sensory data into our sense of external reality. This produces vivid dream-like hallucinations, inhabited by the creatures in question and others equally as fabulous, that the mind cannot distinguish from reality.

Keel thinks the mystery creatures are temporary transmogrifications of this mysterious energy that can sometimes assume objective physicality and that somehow reflect the subconscious contents of the minds of observers.

I will discuss these theories in more detail in a subsequent chapter, but suffice it to say here that the consensus opinion is that there is a link between this energy and the mind, and perhaps with the essential mechanisms of perception. Anytime strange effects on the mind are involved, unusual sightings are thought to be merely subjective. We have seen that this mystery energy can sometimes disrupt electrical systems and may be associated with wild man and other mystery creature sightings.

This suggests that there may at least be a common objective source phenomenon involved. Moreover, the existence of multiple witnesses and the tangibility of footprints and claw marks further suggest that in the creature sightings we are dealing with much more than mere subjective hallucinations.

My nephew, Jeff Leger, told me a story which illustrates another interesting point. He and his dad, Big Jeff, run a crop dusting business that services rice farmers in a large area of Southeast Texas. One of these farmers, who is well-known by Jeff, gave him the following account. He was riding herd horseback on some cattle that he had put out to graze on one of his fields that was left fallow. The field covers several hundred acres and is bordered on one side by thick woods and underbrush that follow the course of a small stream. Before he could find the cattle, his horse began to act up, fidgeting nervously as if it were spooked. He looked up to catch a fleeting glimpse of a large man crouched by a ditch that drains the rice field into the stream.

The man was eating a raw fish with his bare hands. What was so remarkable about the man, the astonished farmer told Jeff, was that he appeared to be naked and to have extremely long black hair. Then it quickly disappeared into the underbrush.

That the animals react nervously in the presence of Ol'Mossyback confirms a pattern we observed earlier. The appearance of a normal person a hundred yards or more away with a normal smell under normal circumstances would not be likely to spook a working farm horse, yet during the entire episode the farmer had to struggle to calm his horse until the mysterious naked man was gone. Except in the unlikely event that the horse was hallucinating like a human would, its reactions are an objective indication that something genuinely out-of-the-ordinary was taking place.

The mysterious link that the lights and energy apparently have with the mind does not force us to dismiss the creature sightings associated with them as induced subjective hallucinations, or even to strongly suspect it. It suggests, rather, that the quality of intense strangeness of the ghost light and its behavior, and that same quality of the wild man and roogaroo manifestations are less matters of superstition than experiences of genuine mystery that may have a common or similar source.

The point here is that something totally outside the range of normal experience and perception is seen with unexpected regularity in wild places in the Big Thicket, the Bayou County, the southern swamplands, and the Northwest mountain forests. Whether in the solid form of ape or primitive human or of a screaming panther, or perhaps dream-like mirages of those forms, the creatures are consistently associated with peculiar ambient energy fields that seem to be part of some kind of mechanism of the strange creatures' appearances. These fields may also produce light-forms that exhibit apparently intelligent behavior. The places where these conditions apply are fairly localized and appearances of both light-forms and creatures have been reported for decades in the same areas. We can be reasonably sure that these same conditions will recur in the same general locations and that the same kinds of experiences and sightings will also continue.

The implications of these facts are enormous. But to underscore the questions they raise about the nature of reality as we like to think we perceive it, we first need to examine the wild man and ghost light legends from another perspective—that of the Native American people. Their traditional perspective is, perhaps, unencumbered with many of the unquestioned assumptions of our modern materialistic culture regarding the nature of reality. From that perspective, the stories from the backwoods of the Big Thicket and the backwaters of Cajun country, far from being easily dismissed as superstitions, are charged with extraordinary possibilities of discovery.

CHAPTER 4

The Indian Mysteries

If the wild man stories are not mere modern folklore, there should be references to the creatures within the traditions and legends of the Native Americans. A brief survey of the literature indicates that this is precisely the case. John Green claims that, "reports of such creatures have been continual, from the original Indian inhabitants of North America and from the explorers and fur traders who invaded the unmapped interior."

Persinger and LaFreniere, whom we cited in previous chapters, report that, "In the years 1917 and 1970, hundreds of people in southwestern Illinois reported seeing large cat-like and humanoid creatures. Along the banks of the Mississippi River, pictures of similar creatures drawn by Indians still exist." Apparently the Indians were also aware of the link between the creatures and mystery lights. Of a tribe of Indians of the Pacific Northwest, researchers Ann Slate and Alan Berry write: "For many years the Yakimas had seen strange lights over the reservation hills and down in the valleys. They had glimpsed the large, foul smelling creature the white man called Bigfoot in their forests and around their campfires. They didn't talk about it to outsiders."

Although the existence of the creatures is acknowledged by Indian traditions since long before the European colonization of the continent, the Indians take a somewhat different view about what the creatures might be than most Western researchers, who generally assume that the ape-man/wild man/Bigfoot/Sasquatch legends are either entirely mythical or are based on sporadic sightings of some kind of undiscovered, perhaps relict, population of rare ape-like animals. Indian traditions, on the other hand, suggest another extremely interesting possibility. According to Hunter and Dahinden, "These reputed hairy creatures are said by Indians to be the remnant of a race who lived on this continent ages ago..." As bizarre as that may sound, a few researchers are beginning to seriously entertain the idea that the sightings are of a remnant population of a pre-homo sapiens human.

"There is some evidence," writes John Keel, "that it might actually be a survivor of the early Neanderthal man. Footprints known to have been made by the Neanderthalers have been discovered and they are almost identical.." Similarly, Boris Porshev, former department chief in the Institute of History of the Academy of Sciences of the former U.S.S.R., was convinced that his evidence indicates the probable existence of "the surviving remains of a branch of the Neanderthals in divers regions of the world," and that this might account for at least some of the Bigfoot type creatures.

To the obvious objection that it would be unlikely that there could be any relict populations of ancient humans inhabiting even the remote areas of the United States without their being easily detected, Hunter and Dahinden point out that it has been only within the last few years, "...that people living in stone-age conditions have been discovered in the Philippines."

These people were no more removed from the urban centers of the Philippines than remote areas in this country, particularly the mountain forests of the Northwest and the swamplands of the Deep South, are removed from our population centers. As we have seen in the preceding chapter, these areas are precisely where most of the large hairy humanoid sightings are reported.

But there may also be another reason why these beings are so elusive. This might not even occur to those of us who are so attached to all our so-called modern conveniences, but these beings, who apparently have had considerable marginal contact with human civilization, may simply not have much use for the way we live. Additionally, they might have enough intelligence and be sufficiently adapted to their environment to make them virtually undetectable in their natural setting. Unless they are unsuspectingly stumbled upon in the wild by hunters or outdoors enthusiasts, or glimpses of them are caught during their nocturnal rounds on the edges of civilization, their very existence might be little suspected.

Andrew Stone believed that something like this was the case and that the Bigfoot were not animals, "but rather, that once, long ago, an Indian band of large stature had chosen to live in the wilds, perhaps underground or in abandoned mines, and slowly evolved strength, speed and hair to adapt to their new environment." Their adaptations may also have included other factors which we would little suspect and which would render them even more undetectable.

We have seen that the wild man creature sightings are associated with the mysterious energies that sometimes manifest as light-forms. These lights, which recur in the same locations for generations in the form of the ghost light phenomenon, also have a peculiar relation to the consciousness of the observer. We have speculated that these energies may be evidence of a form of non-localized consciousness and that as such constitute a sort of field of psychic energy that may be as much a part of our natural environment as the air we breathe.

The wild man/Sasquatch may be so well adapted to this ambient psychic energy field, in evidence in the standing ghost light locations, to have evolved psychic abilities that we can scarcely comprehend. This is entirely consistent with Indian views about the capabilities of the Sasquatch.

John Green notes that "...there are Indian traditions endowing it with psychic power-mind reading, for instance." Hunter and Dahinden wrote of "ancient tales" of the Indians that speak of the creature's "supernatural powers." Slate and Berry, while acknowledging that it is a far-out theory, wrote of "ancient Indian legends and other unorthodox events" during their field research that "led researchers to suspect that the mind of the Bigfoot might indeed possess this telepathic-hypnotic capability."

They go on to cite a number of cases around the country that suggest that, "...the Bigfoot creatures can make themselves invisible, through mind control or delusion of others." Of their own research they say, "There were times when it almost seemed as if the creatures could make themselves invisible, and disappear in a split second. It wasn't a thought that any of the men warmed to or liked to discuss, yet, inexorably, it would surface: were there spiritual or other unknown forces at play?"

Judging from what we have seen about the link of the wild man sightings with the mysterious light-producing energies, there are definitely unknown forces at play. Moreover, these stories and this discussion also shed substantial light on the Cajun legends of the shape-shifting fifolets and on the stories from the Big Thicket about the wild man emerging from the light on Bragg Road. Could they be evidence of a race of beings who have a profound wisdom of subtle energies and their relations to consciousness and perception? Could they use this knowledge in some form of mind control or hypnosis to keep themselves hidden from the view of mankind or to alter the forms they present for our view?

Bigfoot researcher Jack Lapseritis thinks so. Although he initially resisted it, first hand experience from decades of field investigation of sightings compelled him to concede that the phenomenon has bizarre elements that suggest the paranormal. "Most of the sightings of Bigfoot," says Lapseritis, "have been made by hunters and loggers who report being observed by some giant, hairy creature. Several of these reports are of a bizarre nature..." The creatures vanish mysteriously and leave perplexing physical evidence such as footprints and hair. He noted that these types of sightings include reports of strange lights in the sightings areas. He believes the elusive quality of the creatures is related to this bizarre aspect, that it has an interdimensional aspect, and is the key to understanding the phenomenon. This interdimensional aspect enables the creatures to exist and move among more than one "plane of existence in time and space."

James Swan's Sasquatch research among the Indians of the Northwest corroborates much of Lapseritis' conclusions. Swan writes, "A typical Bigfoot sighting involves feeling an unusual active energy in a certain place, often accompanied by a musky odor and a high-pitched scream..." The being then appears and is plainly seen, in some cases may even leave footprints, and then after a short time it simply vanishes. Sun Bear and Rolling Thunder, two medicine men with whom Swan had worked, informed him that these beings were what they called the "old ones" and that they had a very ancient ancestry. Significantly, Swan was also told by Indian medicine men that the hairy ape-like beings live in two worlds and, "...act as guardian spirits of special places and allies of shamans." "Living in two worlds" sounds a lot like what a Native American might say instead of "moving among more than one plane of existence."

If we are to believe the Indian legends, the special quality of places like the Big Thicket and other remote areas the wild man is known to frequent–and to which it acts as a guardian–is that they are focal points where peculiar energy tends to concentrate for reasons unknown. Indeed, it may be the temporary focusing of this energy that makes it possible for the wild man to appear in these particular areas.

If the hairy wild man is a form of ancient man, it has this much in common with the ancient Celts, Britons, Chinese, and certain American Indians. They all placed great importance on knowing when and where these energy spikes would occur. Briefly put, they believed that in such places, under specific energetic conditions, the veil between this and other worlds is removed.

Before you dismiss this as superstitious nonsense, remember that in addition to the bizarre quality of the wild man's appearances and vanishings, the behavior exhibited by the ghost lights, both in terms of their "consciousness" and in how long they maintain discrete form, does not fit any pattern of the laws of thermodynamics as we know them, nor can they be duplicated in the laboratory. This forces us to seriously consider the startling possibility that the conditions necessary to produce these lights amounts to a temporary suspension of certain laws in the physical universe. Under these conditions who knows what is possible?

In the modern age we have become, for the most part, unconscious of this energy. In a few remote locations, in places like the Big Thicket, the Louisiana Bayou Country, and the forested mountains of the Northwest, there still exist points where the energies can focus enough for us to be conscious of them despite our ignorance and neglect. As we will discuss subsequently in greater detail, it may be that the wildness of these places is a necessary element allowing these energies to focus there. The subtle negative environmental effects of increasing urbanization and our growing estrangement from the natural world may be the main reasons we have become largely unconscious of an essential part of Nature through which we can connect to that which is beyond the normal limitations of consciousness.

According to Indian legend and tradition, the Bigfoot or wild man does not suffer from the ignorance of this energy and the opportunities it may afford. From the stories we have heard and the considerations we have entertained it appears the creature has extraordinary capabilities. It may possess a practical and usable knowledge of the subtle relation between consciousness and the structure of reality that suggests that the "observer-created" universe theory of quantum physics is more than speculation.

A portrait emerges, then, from Native American lore of the wild, hairy ape-man. It is more human than animal and is descended from an ancient and large-bodied people that, like the Indians themselves, is indigenous to this continent from remote antiquity. Its physical stature is of near gigantic proportions and it may approach or exceed seven feet in height. It is primitive in appearance and has adapted and attuned itself to certain subtle energies within the natural environment.

It has knowledge of when and where these subtle energies periodically intensify and is able to consciously and physically enter other realities when the energy spikes rend the fabric of this world and make the other worlds accessible. Its psychic attunement to these subtle energies also gives it the ability to read the minds of others and to be able to make itself invisible, perhaps by entering the minds of others and altering what they perceive. From a combination of this ability with its mental powers, it is seen to make sudden and unexpected appearances and likewise to disappear mysteriously. It is likely that the wild man's numerous appearances on Bragg Road are due to its attraction to this same type of energy that sometimes manifests there as ghost lights.

During one of our photo sessions on the ghost road, Bill and I might have indirectly gained some insight into the wild man's ability to make itself invisible and also perhaps into its limitations. We had been there for hours, hoping to capture the ghost light on film, and occasionally visiting with other ghost light hunters who stopped by out of curiosity when they saw our tripod setup. After visits from two different truckloads of teenagers, who after swapping stories and observations with us, headed off in opposite directions up and down Bragg Road, we were alone keeping our vigil. Our visits with these kids had added up to just more than an hour. During that time we had been sitting on the side of the road just above a shallow ditch that separated the roadbed from the thick woods that border the road. About 45 minutes later, both truckloads returned to our location at exactly the same time from opposite directions.

Nothing unusual or suspicious had occurred between these visits. There were no unusual noises, either on the road or from the surrounding woods. Just when the two truckloads arrived–simultaneously, as it happens–something massive took off noisily into the woods, not more than five or ten feet from where we had been staked out for nearly two hours. Was it perhaps startled and suddenly exposed by the unexpected arrival of the two trucks? We didn't have time to see what it was before it vanished. Bill was holding a flashlight at the time, but he ignored my excited urging that he should go off running into the woods to try to identify whatever it was. He wondered whether I would have been so brave if I had been the one holding the flashlight. Whatever it was, it was also very fast and was quickly out of audible range as it crashed through the swampy muck and the palmetto fronds.

My first thought was that it could have been an armadillo. But if it had been an armadillo, which was about the only wild animal I could think of that would be stupid enough to venture that close to us, we would have heard it coming from a long way off. Armadillos are notoriously clumsy and are stupidly oblivious of their surroundings. This is why you see so many of them flattened out on Texas highways and why nature has equipped them with armor. They would otherwise be totally defenseless. Also, if it had been a 'dillo, we would have seen it before it disappeared. They just can't move as fast as whatever this was.

What spooked us was that this thing was big and we had never seen or heard it approach us. For all we knew it could have been observing us for some time. How could something apparently so large have done that? How could we have not seen this thing? It had to have been between us and the edge of the woods, which was ten to fifteen feet away, and therefore plainly visible even in the darkness. And why did it take off so suddenly when the two trucks arrived?

Whatever went crashing into the woods might have made itself invisible to us. In much the same way the luminous mist or fog, which showed up on the film that Bill and I took on Bragg Road, was never visible to us. In a following chapter we will discuss in greater detail how the wild man may be tapping into an ambient, non-localized field of conscious energy and entering into the mind of its observers. But could there be a limit on how many people it can affect at any one time? Did it have to take off when the number of people who suddenly arrived put the total number over the limit for it to maintain hidden from our view?

With powers like this, which the Native Americans recognize, the wild man may be the guardian of the special places where these rare energetic conditions occur. The wild man is said to ward off those whom happenstance might place in the vicinity of such places, whether to its advantage or to the benefit of those who might be unprepared to deal with the energies. It may also act as an ally to human shamans who seek access to these other worlds.

One other quality sometimes attributed to the wild man completes the portrait in a most disturbing manner. Some traditions hold that the wild man has been known to consume human flesh. Hunter and Dahinden cited Paul Kane and his research among the

Indians of the Mount St. Helens area in the1840s: "This mountain has never been visited by either whites or Indians; the latter assert that it is inhabited by a race of beings of a different species, who are cannibals, and whom they hold in great dread." Washington state, of course, has had many Sasquatch sightings on up to the present day.

Is there folklore about Sasquatch among the Indians of Southeast Texas? Is there anything within the lore or the history of Indians of the area that would fit the portrait of the wild man–an ancient, perhaps very primitive form of human of huge stature, given to at least occasional cannibalism, and perhaps endowed with unusual powers?

The largest of only three Indian reservations left in Texas is adjacent to the northernmost unit of the Big Thicket National Preserve. The Alabama and Coushatta tribes have called it home since before the days of the Republic of Texas. A Preserve ranger told me that there have been sightings of the wild man in that general area of Polk County. These sightings are recent, however, and there is no indication that the wild man is any more a part of Alabama-Coushatta folklore than that of the region in general.

There is little extant Indian folklore of indigenous tribes of any type in the Big Thicket region. Fortunately, this is not, as in most parts of Texas, because the original inhabitants of the area have been removed or exterminated. It seems that the Indians, for the most part, avoided the depths of the Thicket.

Texas historian Howard N. Martin concluded that only two groups of Indians associated with the Thicket or moved through the area with any regularity prior to the resettling of the Alabama-Coushattas at the end of the eighteenth century. Occasionally, hunting parties from tribes as far away as Oklahoma and Kansas made hunting trips to the Thicket for bear meat, skins, and tallow, according to Martin, "and Tonkawas, Lipans, and Wichitas met in peace at the medicinal springs around present-day Sour Lake and Saratoga." But "primarily the Thicket was the meat house" of the mound-building Caddoes whose home was in the fertile rolling hills to the north of the Thicket, and the Atakapans who lived outside the southern and southeastern boundaries of the Thicket on the Gulf Coast and in the Trinity river bottoms swamp. These two tribes probably maintained the closest permanent settlements to the heart of the Big Thicket.

Even these tribes were limited in their access to certain parts of the Thicket. And according to Campbell and Lynn Loughmiller, the editors of *Big Thicket Legacy*, even though the tribes were attracted by abundant game, they "could penetrate portions of this primeval wilderness only by canoe..." They are said also to have avoided the impenetrable tangle of the deep woods, and in Big Thicket guide Lance Rosier's words, "A lot of this country was so thick that the Indians couldn't get through it..." In general, from the relative lack of significant archaeological sites, it is not clear that any tribes maintained a continuous existence in the traditional heart of the Thicket in western and northwestern Hardin County.

Scholars speculate that the indigenous Indians avoided the depths of the traditional Thicket due to their superstitious belief that it was inhabited by evil demons. If the creature and mystery light sightings that recur to this day in Hardin County are any indication, the Indians' fears might well have been justified.

But at least one tribe might not have avoided the ghost light areas of the Thicket, and indeed may have actually had specific reason to go there. Significantly, individuals of this tribe bore enough resemblance to the Indians' description of the wild man and did so to such a degree as to provide us with some intriguing clues to the wild man's origin, nature and mystery.

In the introduction to his *Tales from the Big Thicket*, Francis

Abernethy writes that the Thicket was relatively uninhabited even by the Indians until well into the nineteenth century. Prior to that time it served as a hide-out and refuge for those who needed to make themselves scarce for awhile.

Abernethy points out that Sam Houston had planned to retreat to and hide his army in the Big Thicket woods if he had lost to Santa Ana's forces at the Battle of San Jacinto. In discussing the original settlers who moved to the area in the decades immediately following the Texas Revolution, Abernethy points out that, "not all of these settlers that moved into the Thicket in the 1840's and 1850's were going there because they liked mosquitoes; some of them were hiding out." Ironically, among those who sought refuge in the Thicket at that time, according to Abernethy, were, "the last of the Atakapans and some of the Karankawas who were being run off their traditional hunting grounds..."

Both of these tribes fit that most disturbing criterion of how the wild man is typically characterized by the Indians—both practiced cannibalism. The Karankawas, or Karanks, as they were also called, also pass muster on a number of other key points of comparison.

Consider this portrait of the Karanks from *Cannibal Coast* by Ed Kilman. The Tonkawas called them the "Barefooted" or "Without Moccasins" tribe, and both they and the white settlers "shrank at the sight of the huge toed-in footprints" of the man-eating Karanks in the sands and marshes along the Gulf Coast. Kilman goes on to say that the Karanks "towered as giants among savages of ordinary stature, magnificent physical specimens, but facially hideous." Adult males were said to regularly reach up to seven feet in height. Their repugnance to the whites and other Indians was enhanced by tattooing of the face and torso. They usually went naked and barefoot and "wore only a coating of smelly shark oil or alligator grease, sometimes mixed with dirt, to repel mosquitoes." From this they gained the reputation of always carrying a terrible stench.

This stench also evoked horror among their enemies as their odor was a sure giveaway of their impending approach. There was another habit of the Karanks that struck terror in the hearts of their enemies. They were known for their prolonged, loud, almost animal-like eerie howls.

This should sound familiar by now. The large bare feet, the awful stench, the towering height, the terrifying howl–on these points at least the description of the Karank is almost identical to that of the Bigfoot or wild man. But what of the hairy body that is always attributed to the ape-like creatures? Although the Karanks were typically seen as bare-skinned and virtually naked, they apparently sometimes wore skins about their waists and covered themselves with animal pelts in cold weather. They also had waist length shiny black hair. Imagine catching a fleeting glimpse of a Karanakawa warrior in the dim and scattered light of the deep forest. You have just been overcome by his lack of super strength deodorant and have probably also had your nerves shattered by his ear-splitting howl. The combination of animal skins, tattoos, and mud smeared over most of his body and his long, shaggy mane could well give the impression that he was completely covered with shaggy black hair.

Does this "explain" the wild man mystery? I think it gets pretty close. There is one more compelling parallel between the wild man and the Karanks that almost completes the matching portraits. Kilman notes that there is considerable discussion among scholars that "…the Karankawas may have been related to the prehistoric Abilene Man." Is this, then, the fearsome ancient form of man of which Indian legends speak? The Karankawas dropped out of the historical scene almost two hundred years ago.

Is it possible that isolated populations could still exist?

Some researchers have considered this a possibility. Hunter and Dahinden, in their discussion of the Indian belief that the Sasquatch are remnants of an ancient indigenous race, make note of the primitive nature and huge stature of the Karanks. Even though there has been no recognized trace of them for some time, they speculate "whether they found their way to the Northwest, and in sufficient numbers to propagate their race until the present time."

Even if we allow for this possibility–no matter how remote–it still leaves us with one piece missing from the puzzle, perhaps the most important piece. What of the wild man's mysterious powers? Is there any evidence that the Karanks exhibited such powers? Ed Kilman in *Cannibal Coast* reports on some Karankawa shamanic beliefs and practices that may be relevant to this question. Kilman says that they made tea from the berries of the wild yaupon to induce visions. During their trances a "guiding spirit" was supposed to occupy the young brave's shadow and to "attend him all the days of his life." Could the spirit have been the wild man?

We have already noted that some Indian traditions hold that the Sasquatch is a spirit being capable of physical manifestation who guards places of special power. Under some circumstances it would also act as an ally to tribal shamans. Could the Karankawa shamans have entered into a profound mental, perhaps psychic, link with the hairy wild creature that would have affected their behavior and combined with their physical stature to make them even more similar to their spirit allies? Along with the tribe's warriors, they might also have deliberately emulated the wild man's behavior and appearance, especially in their howling and animal skin coverings, in a totemistic imitation of the wild man intended to imbue them with the wild man's nature and powers.

They may have learned from the Sasquatch the secrets of

when and where cyclical energy conditions would open doors to other realities. If their shamans had mastered the art of "living in two worlds" and were able to teach it to the rest of the tribe, it could account for the Karankawa's sudden and mysterious disappearance that has baffled historians for well over a hundred years. It could also account for why the last of the Karankawas' dwindling population apparently sought refuge in the heart of the Big Thicket, a place that was strictly avoided by other tribes.

If the Karanks were, indeed, in league with the hairy wild men, they may have been as attracted to the energy "springs" of the ghost light area as other tribes were drawn to the mineral springs near present-day Sour Lake and Saratoga. The Tonkawas, Caddoes and the rest sought cures for their ailments from the medicinal powers of the smelly sulfur water. With the wild men acting as their allies, the Karanks may have sought assistance, not only in their shamanic practices, but also in their flight from European encroachment. If Hunter and Dahinden's theory that the Karankawas abandoned their original homeland for the Pacific Northwest is tenable, how much more likely is it that they would have stayed much closer to home in the Big Thicket? If Bigfoot sightings in the Northwest could possibly be attributed to the Karanks, how much more so could the Big Thicket wild man sightings, especially in light of what we have discussed, be attributable to them?

What are we to conclude at this point? There definitely seem to be ape-like creatures seen not infrequently in the Big Thicket. These are not likely to be cases of Karankawa warriors being mistaken for hairy monsters. The shamanic connection between the two is a more likely scenario, for there are two types of sightings reported that bear on this matter, and both contain elements of strange energy disturbances. If there actually are Karanks still living in the Big Thicket and surrounding area, and they are similar in appearance but distinct from the wild man creatures, what kind of sightings stories would they be likely to produce?

A friend who had heard of my research introduced me to Rick (who asked that his last name not be used), a professional treasure hunter from the Texas Gulf Coast. Rick has spent years exploring the Gulf of Mexico and the Caribbean searching for lost Spanish gold. One of the tools of his trade is a magnetometer which he uses like an over-sized metal detector to survey from the air the areas that he considers promising. The device reveals anomalies in the magnetic field, some of which could be caused by large deposits of metal, such as would be contained in a buried treasure. This technique is particularly effective in swampy areas of the Texas Gulf Coast, which contain little natural metal-bearing stone or ore.

During a survey of the lower Trinity Valley swamp not far north of Trinity Bay, an arm of Galveston Bay, Rick discovered just such an anomalous spot. He knew the area was the subject of legends of buried treasure, so he was encouraged by the magnetometer reading and quickly prepared to explore the site on foot. When he was approaching the site, he happened to meet a game warden. The game warden noticed that he was not carrying hunting or fishing equipment and asked where he was going. When Rick told him, the game warden asked Rick to reconsider.

Several hunters and fishermen had been attacked in the area Rick wanted to investigate. The game warden believed these reports because he had been attacked himself. Naturally, Rick wanted to know who would be that hostile and what his motive might be. At this point, Rick said, the warden looked at him as if trying to weigh in his mind whether Rick would believe him or think he was nuts.

An "Indian," the warden said, had attacked him, narrowly missing him with an arrow. At least that's who he thought his attacker was. Although he didn't get a long look at him, his assailant was big, practically naked, dark, and visibly upset that someone was trespassing on his territory. Rick wondered aloud what kind of weirdo would be wandering the swamp playing Indian, and even if it were an Indian, why would it be attacking hunters with bow and arrow when it ought to know that it might receive return fire from a deer rifle.

Rick wasn't sure that the game warden still possessed the arrow that was shot at him, but the game warden claimed that he had examined it closely and that it was not a modern-type arrow like what you would buy at a sporting goods store. It appeared to be hand-made, a genuine artifact and primitive. That term would also best describe the Indian's appearance, as well. There was something strange about the Indian, he said, that could only be described as very primitive, as if he was not from our time.

Rick didn't get the game warden's name, he merely thought the incident curious at the time, and the arrow in question, as far as I know, could not be produced. This should not, however, lead us to entirely dismiss this story as mere hearsay. Again we have the simultaneous occurrence of a strong localized magnetic anomaly and the appearance of a strange and out-of-place humanoid. This incident, by the way, occurred not far from the site of the Route Monster sightings, and it is not an isolated story. A corroborating story from an entirely independent source came to me from Eddie Ramirez, one of my students when I was teaching English in Beaumont.

Eddie's mom had a cabin, which she used for weekend retreats and fishing trips, in a remote fish camp off the lower Trinity River near Trinity Bay. This was the same general area of Rick's treasure hunting experience. An old man who ran a small store and bait shop in the area told her the following story. An electrical utility lineman had been sent to a remote area bordering the swamp to make repairs. After he had made the repairs and was ready to climb down from the utility pole, he was startled to find that the base of the pole was surrounded by what he described as several "Indians." They glared at him menacingly for awhile before disappearing into the surrounding woods. The lineman noticed that they were practically naked and appeared to be very primitive; they were brandishing what seemed to be equally primitive weapons, including bows. Why they didn't shoot at him is anyone's guess.

Admittedly, this is a fourth-hand story and as such smacks of hearsay, but there are yet again elements of the story that suggest some familiar patterns. Why was the repairman sent to that area? Could there have been a localized power outage caused by the same kind of intense local magnetic anomaly that led Rick to search the same area for buried treasure?

The old man at the bait shop thought enough of the story to investigate the area, but he was quickly discouraged from continuing his search by a horrifying discovery. He found the skeletal remains of a human strapped to the base of a tree not far from where the lineman had seen the Indians.

As fantastic and as hard to believe as this last bit of information was, there was also a haunting familiarity to it. There actually was a tribe of Indians on the Texas Gulf Coast, thought to have disappeared in the early 1800s, who performed a brutal ceremony with anyone unfortunate enough to be captured by one of their war parties. They strapped their captive to a tree, and subjected him to a prolonged and agonizing death by stripping the flesh from his body. They roasted the flesh before their victim's eyes in a bonfire around which they danced in a frenzied stupor induced by drinking a potion made from yaupon berries. You've already read about them in this narrative. That tribe was the Karankawas.

More recent sightings of what are described as primitive

Indians further corroborate these stories. Tom Dillman, a Houston businessman and amateur treasure hunter, provided yet another independent source relating to possible surviving Karankawas on the Texas coast. Tom was beach combing near the mouth of Trinity Bay with his metal-detector when by chance he met another prospector whom he knew from previous outings. Tom mentioned that he would like to take an air boat upstream from the mouth of the bay into the swamps and bayous that empty into the Trinity River to look for a legendary pirate ship that is said to have shipwrecked long ago in that area.

The other prospector told Tom that if he did so he should take extra precautions. He knew of people who had been attacked by Indians there. Tom asked why the victims thought they had been attacked by Indians rather than by a bunch of drug-crazed 1960's survivalist hippies. Because they had been attacked by bow and arrow, the man said, and the arrows, and the Indians themselves, were very primitive looking. There was also the matter of their scent. They reeked so badly from smearing themselves with some kind of putrefied animal fat that you could smell them coming from some distance away. Tom knew enough of Karankawa lore to know that they covered themselves in alligator or shark grease to protect themselves from the clouds of mosquitoes that permanently infest the swamps.

Significantly, Tom related his story to me before he had heard of my other Karankawas stories. He also had no idea how many details in his account paralleled those of the stories told by Rick and Eddie.

There was yet another story that may have involved a Karankawa sighting. A lady from Saratoga told me that some male members of her family had gone hunting somewhere along the Little Pine Island Bayou. They had just come around a bend in the stream opening up to a relatively unobstructed view along a good stretch of water, and were stunned at the sudden appearance of a large, almost naked "Indian" in a rough-hewn wooden dugout boat. As in the other stories, what impressed them most was the extremely primitive appearance of the Indian.

Perhaps it was the overall incongruity of seeing something so out-of-place and out-of-time, or maybe it was the extreme sense of strangeness that wild man and ghost light sightings engender, but for whatever reason the men were not of a mood to investigate. The experience spooked them and they made a hurried retreat from the area. The Karanks, by the way, are said to have used dugout pirouge boats in the coastal waters and streams of the Texas Gulf Coast.

Clearly, the wild man sightings cannot be taken as cases of mistaken identity of what are actually sightings of Karankawas. There seem to be two distinctly different types of sightings. The overlaps and similarities of the two are intriguing, though, especially because, in some cases at least, the Indian sightings include the same signature energy anomaly characteristic of the wild man sightings.

If you are of a mind to go tromping off into the swamp to make what would easily be the anthropological discovery of the century, hold your horses. Aside from the possible danger of being attacked by someone who might be able to see you while remaining invisible to your senses, consider this. As in the case of the wild man, an expedition to the Thicket or the Trinity bottom swamps would probably reveal no existing populations of surviving Karankawas.

This does not mean, however, that they have not been seen in the present time and that the stories have no basis in reality. These sightings are not common enough for the observers to have been influenced by either media reports or a widely established folklore of such sightings. In the light of all that we have seen about the strange energies involved, there must be something genuinely unusual giving rise to these stories. The Karanks may only exist, however, as transient phenomena in the same way the wild man does. They may only be able to make appearances when the periodic energy intensifications are activated by employing the same mechanisms we have considered in the wild man and ghost light occurrences. Even if you were lucky enough to happen to go to an area where these energies might occur at a time when they are active, that would still not assure you of seeing a wild man or a Karank, unless they wanted you to.

We are dealing with something most of us are totally ignorant of, and with areas of the mind with which we are unfamiliar. That would put you at a decided disadvantage in any possible confrontation with beings who may know of these strange energies and the mental powers and perceptual effects associated with them.

To put the profound implications of the Karankawa sightings into perspective and to illustrate how they might only be accounted for within a worldview that's alien to the typical Western common sense materialistic model of reality, I would like you to consider one more Indian tradition–that of the Hopi.

Bill and I were scheduled to meet with representatives of the Hopi while en route to make a presentation at a symposium on the "Spirit of Place" hosted by James Swan at Cal State Fullerton. Bill had called ahead to make an appointment for us to meet a gentleman who claimed to be the Hopi spokesman. When we arrived, we soon found that we were no longer on white man standard time and that he was nowhere to be found. His wife informed us that he had business elsewhere and she had no idea when he would return. We politely asked her if we could come back the next day. She agreed, but offered no assurance that he would be there then either.

When we returned the next morning, we found him still absent. We asked if we could wait for him. The lady seemed surprised that we would choose that option, probably assuming that since we were not Hopi we would be in a hurry. We sat on lawn chairs in her back yard for several hours and it soon became obvious that she was not interested in casual conversation. After awhile, though, she graciously offered us refreshments, and seemed to relax a bit. It didn't occur to us at the time that we were being tested, but she seemed impressed by our patience. Gradually she became openly curious about our intentions and allowed herself to be pulled into conversation.

From what I knew about Hopi tradition, I suspected that many of the same unusual luminous and mystery creature phenomena that recur in the Big Thicket area might also occur in the Hopi lands. Over the next few hours, she described multiple incidences of three phases of luminous phenomena that have been seen from time immemorial by the Hopi.

People had spoken to her of star-like objects that moved through the sky in geometrical patterns, streaking at great speed, making impossible right angle turns without slowing down, and then sometimes tracing the diagonals of the right angles they had just made. Numerous sightings of the large orange-colored fireballs that have been witnessed a number of times streaking through the sky above the Thicket are duplicated in the Hopi lands. There were also areas she knew of where smaller globes of bluish-white light would approach witnesses at ground level in events that reminded me of episodes of the ghost light on Bragg Road.

But the lady wouldn't elaborate much on her descriptions and wouldn't introduce us to any of the witnesses. Her people didn't much like to talk about such things to outsiders she said. Nonetheless, from what she did tell us, the same electromagnetic anomaly conditions that occur in the Thicket region are likely to happen in the Hopi's ancestral lands as well.

If the Big Thicket light phenomena are duplicated there, what of the mystery creatures? John Green writes of a legendary creature seen by the Hopi and Navajo on their reservations since antiquity and called the "skin walker." Green thinks this may be a Bigfoot-type creature.

The Hopi also have a tradition of what they call the Kachina or spirit beings. The Kachina are a form of personified nature spirits, and there are literally hundreds of them corresponding to all forms of nature including things like wind, sun, rain, and so on. Originally references to them were more specific. They were said to be a race of beings of near gigantic proportions (eight feet in height) that came from their home in the nearby San Francisco peaks to charge the Hopi with a specific mission.

They told the Hopi that for eons the Kachina had the duty of keeping the world in balance, and that responsibility was to pass from them to the Hopi people. The Kachina taught the Hopi the rituals, prayers, and ceremonies necessary to keep the world in balance, and then the Kachina departed for their home at the center of the universe. They promised the Hopi that they would return for them one day to take the Hopi to the Kachina's home at the center of the universe.

One Kachina is graphically and symbolically depicted in Hopi ceremonial dolls as a large, hairy man-like being with enough similarity to the Sasquatch/ wild man to suggest that there may be a relation between them and the early references to a race of eight foot tall spirit beings. The myth of the Kachina's leaving for their home in the center of the universe may be related to the notion of spirit beings living in two worlds. This is made more likely by another element of Hopi mythology that might help us understand the magnitude of what confronts us in these places where unusual energy become periodically intense.

We have seen that the Indians of the Northwest believe that the Sasquatch is a being capable of passing from one world to another and that this capability is more than likely linked with these same energy intensities. We have also speculated that when these energies are in effect they might temporarily suspend certain laws of the physical universe in highly localized areas with unpredictable results, possibly including the window area phenomenon described by John Keel. Though this may sound fantastic, science does speak of conditions under which the normal perceptible order of things does not apply.

The warping, or curvature, of space caused by intense gravitational or magnetic fields, worm holes that provide short cuts between vastly distant points in linear space, multiple dimensions of space, and the reverse flow of time, have all long been held as being theoretically, and to varying degrees experimentally, possible. It is normally assumed, however, that these exotic conditions, if they ever exist at all, do so on a vast scale at the far end of the galaxy, or on such a minute scale on the sub-atomic level, that they have no bearing on actual human experience.

The Hopi tradition also contains a reference to what could be thought of as a state or condition outside normal space-time. It is called the sipapuni, or the hole in the earth. It is represented in their kivas, or circular ceremonial lodges, and has come to have a spiritual significance, but it is more than a symbolic reference. The sipapuni is the hole in the earth, the place of emergence, through which the Hopi came from elsewhere and emerged into this world. It would be a mistake to dismiss the sipapuni as a naive, pre-scientific religious belief.

According to Frank Waters, author of *The Book of the Hopi,* it refers to the earth's magnetic field and a shift of the polar center from a "now vanished Third World" to the "present Fourth

World." We have just seen that the characteristic phenomena associated with periodic magnetic anomalies of great intensity occur in the Hopi land. An intimate knowledge of these energies and their effects on consciousness, and indeed on the fabric of reality, may have given the Hopi, or at least the present-day Hopi's ancestors, an understanding of the nature and structure of space and time that would be totally alien to the typical modern Westerner. It may also have given them access to a dimension of physical space, made available by the warping or curvature of space from immense energy intensities, that would not exist for those whose cultural reality map would prevent them from understanding the full dimensionality of space. If this sounds far-fetched, we have an example, or at least a corollary, from Western history of how the widespread ignorance of the dimensionality of space prevented access to a greater world.

In the European world of Columbus' day the dominant cosmological paradigm, the way in which the world was seen and understood, was that the earth was basically two-dimensional or flat. This ignorance of the curvature of space made the notion of the Earth as a sphere incomprehensible. There may have been learned philosophers in the universities who understood something of the earth's sphericity, but this was regarded as mere theory. The idea of actually putting the theory to the test by sailing around the earth was regarded as hopelessly romantic at best, if not impractical and an obvious affront to common sense

This is not to romanticize Columbus' intentions, for they were as much fueled by greed and avarice as anything else, but when he completed his voyage he did more than expand the map. He had to first overcome a view of the world, which lacked in an understanding of the full dimensionality of space, and in which the very idea of the lands he discovered would not even exist.

We could also imagine a situation in which an entire people

who did understand the curvature and sphericity of the earth, could leave Europe and sail to America and be thought of by the ignorant to have simply vanished or fallen off the face of the earth, when in fact they would simply be living in another space that would be incomprehensible to the uneducated.

This point may give us a clue, not only to the nature of the sipapuni, but to another mystery of the Karankawas. At one time, although their numbers were never large, the Karakawas had a thriving culture along the Texas Gulf Coast. One of their largest settlements was said to have been near the present-day city of Beaumont near the mouth of the Neches River on the eastern edge of the Big Thicket. After being the scourge of the other Native Americans with whom they competed for territory and the terror of the few Europeans who had dared the rigors of settling an extreme and hostile environment, the Karanks abruptly exited the scene. Historically speaking, they simply disappeared around the turn of the 19th century just as Texas was about to see a great influx of European settlers.

Historians disagree on the cause of their disappearance. There was no great defeat in battle or epidemic on record that would have quickly depleted their numbers. Famine is very unlikely, since there was always an abundance of fish in the bays and estuaries that were their favored habitat. There was no recorded exodus or trail of tears-type exile for these fearsome warriors. Perhaps it is no coincidence that they disappeared just as the Europeans were beginning to arrive. We have already noted that one researcher thinks they may have made their way to the Pacific Northwest and that they may account for the Bigfoot sightings. Another possibility is that they retreated to a space, made accessible to them from the factors we have considered, of which the Europeans were unaware.

The Karankawas' sudden disappearance is not an isolated

occurrence among ancient Native American cultures. Similar events have been noted among the Anasazi, Toltec, Maya, Hopewellian, and Nagualists cultures. A full anthropological treatment of this topic is beyond the scope of this work. As we shall see, however, besides the occurrence of mysterious sudden disappearances, there are indications that all of these cultures may have shared at least some elements of the same fundamental knowledge of the earth's subtle energies. These cultures may also have employed a technology that predicted and utilized periodic natural energy intensities that gave them access to what the Hopi called sipapuni. By this means they may have been able to enter spaces that would be unimaginable to us.

If this sounds a bit outlandish, may I remind you that the existence of other dimensions of space has long been held to be mathematically and theoretically possible. It is astonishing to think that the hole in the earth could be more than speculative philosophy or a mathematical equation, or that one could have conscious access to it. This may be particularly difficult to comprehend because we do not appreciate the relation between consciousness and a so-called external, objectively real world.

In the view of shamanic traditional peoples like the Native Americans, and in such great philosophic and spiritual traditions as Hinduism and Buddhism, matter is not regarded as primary to the existence of conscious life. Rather, conscious being is thought of as primary to external reality. The apparently objective world, and the matter that composes it, are thought of as reflecting the minds of conscious beings. This notion is actually quite in agreement with the observer-created universe theory of quantum physics in which matter does not exist apart from the act of perception by the observer. Within this worldview, a hole in the earth–objectively affecting the very structure of space and time–would be more understandable and would not just be a subjective or imaginary state of mind.

The existence of such a hole in the earth would pose some interesting questions. The Karankawas didn't just disappear from the stage of history. As we have seen, apparently they also show up again from time to time, at least for brief intervals. Is it possible then to cross back and forth through the hole in the earth? Are there warps in time as well as in space? Are the Karanks and the wild men who appear in recent times the same ones who disappeared, in the case of the Karanks centuries ago, and in the case of the wild men possibly thousands of years ago? Can conscious beings of the past and present exist at the same place and moment and be aware of one another?

But again a full-scale expedition to the Big Thicket or the Trinity River swamps would not be likely to turn up a wild man or a displaced primitive Indian, even if the energy conditions necessary for their being able to appear in this world were active. Under these circumstances, would it be possible for an ordinary person to inadvertently stumble and fall into another dimension of space or another time, or is it more likely that accessing the hole in the earth requires the conscious participation of an observer?

In the next chapter we will discuss how the paranormal events described in this book and similar phenomena reported and catalogued by observers and researchers worldwide address these issues, and may be indicators of the inadequacies of our notions of space and time. Assuming that the energetic conditions necessary to manifest as a sipapuni, or hole in the earth, sometimes exist in the Big Thicket and other places where the mystery lights and mystery creatures appear, how exactly might we recognize such a place?

CHAPTER 5

The Hole in the Earth

"I also believe that the lovely round shape of the earth is only the second rough approximation of its form, the flat shape having been our first." So wrote Jacques Bergier, co-author with Louis Pauwels of the classic, *Morning of the Magicians,* in his less well-known but equally intriguing work, *Secret Doors of the Earth.* How could the true geometry of the earth not be the simple sphere, as is widely accepted, Bergier asks?

To fully answer this question, Bergier says, would involve complicated mathematics: "But let's say for the record that mathematicians know of what they call the Riemann surfaces, composed of a great many layers. These layers are neither one on top of the other nor one under the other. They occupy very simply the same space, a space more complex than we usually conceive of space as being..."

If the earth's surface conforms to this more complex space, he says, "...as fantastic as this may seem it's possible that there are unknown and normally inaccessible regions, found neither on a map nor on a globe, which yet exist in reality." He further speculates that "these other regions of the universe" would have "points of contact" that open on to our world through what he calls "secret doors."

Bergier speculates that places likely to contain a secret door share certain characteristics: gravity is disturbed, terrestrial magnetism is disrupted, visions occur to visitors at the site; and enigmatic disappearances take place. Due to the brain's response to magnetic or gravitational disturbances, witnesses in such a place may "sometimes have the impression of being pulled backwards by powerful hands."

Stan and I experienced something like this peculiar sense of disorientation one night on Bragg Road. We were parked across the far northern end of the Kountze-Honey Island highway and faced south down the full length of the ghost road. We had been sitting there for some time, when I suddenly felt like the car was moving. Before I could say anything to Stan, he also felt it and actually hit his brakes to stop the car, but the car had not actually been moving. For a few seconds we both felt like some invisible force was pulling us back down the road, even though we knew the car was not really moving.

You might be familiar with a comparable sensation called undertow. If you have ever stood on the beach where the surf reaches just past your feet before it recedes back into the ocean, you may feel that there is a great force pulling you back toward the open water. This same sensation of movement, even though there actually is none, was described to me by a number of witnesses who experienced it just before they saw the ghost light on Bragg Road.

I have already documented disruptions of terrestrial magnetism in the Big Thicket region. But besides the appearance of the ghost lights and mystery creatures and the occurrence of electrical disturbances and blackouts, what other recognizable effects might these magnetic disruptions have?

In 1995 Stan and I decided to make a spur-of-the-moment trip to Bragg Road on the occasion of the Spring equinox. Such cultures as the Celts, who were more attuned to nature than we are, also attached importance to the equinoxes and solstices, so we thought it might be interesting to be on Bragg Road at the precise moment the equinox occurred. Stan calculated that the exact time would be about 2:30 a.m. We timed our four and a half hour drive from Austin to arrive at Bragg Road a little after 2:00 a.m.

We drove a couple of miles up from the south end of the road to where a pipeline right-of-way intersects it and got out of the car. This gave us a north-south-east-west axis from which to view the sky; it would otherwise have been obstructed by the heavy woods that surround the area.

After about an hour it dawned on me that we were experiencing something remarkable. No, we didn't see the ghost light or anything that could be remotely mistaken for it. In fact, there was no sign of anything on Bragg Road or anywhere in the vicinity. I asked Stan to be quiet and listen and tell me what he heard. He said that he heard nothing. And that, I pointed out, was what was so remarkable.

There we were, in the midst of a vast swampland, inhabited by untold thousands of insects and frogs of every description, by numerous nocturnal mammals including coyotes, and by several different species of night-hunting owls, and for at least an hour we had heard exactly nothing; not one buzz, not one hoot, not one howl, not one croak, not one screech. In all my years in those woods I had never experienced such a thing. All around us was stone dead silence. Even the soothing, ever-present sound of wind blowing through the treetops was absent. It was as quiet and as creepy as a tomb. We just soaked in the weird, penetrating silence.

Stan had postulated that part of the attraction of the energy that produces the ghost light on Bragg Road might have to do with the road's straightness and its alignment. The road is almost eight miles long, is arrow straight and runs almost exactly north and south. We decided to check to see if it's aligned with magnetic north. Stan pulled out his compass and we watched as the needle bobbed. When it finally came to rest, it pointed at a perpendicular to the line of the road–due east. Stan had no sooner questioned the accuracy of my knowledge of the road's north-south direction than the needle began to slowly spin counter-clockwise. We stood there and watched in amazement for several minutes and the needle never stopped spinning. Obviously, we were being subjected to very unusual magnetic conditions for a compass to malfunction in this way. Could these same conditions have also silenced the insects and wildlife of the area?

Unusual magnetic conditions resulting in compass malfunc-tionings are not uncommon in the Lance Rosier Unit of the Big Thicket National Preserve. A well known and respected Big Thicket guide from Kountze once told me that there is at least one spot in that part of the Thicket, which is curiously void of vegeta-tion, where he has seen a compass act in the same bizarre manner we had witnessed on Bragg Road. Rangers at the Preserve head-quarters in Beaumont also told me that they frequently need to rescue hunters who get lost in the Thicket during deer season because their compasses fail them.

Could the Big Thicket harbor a "secret door" that Bergier talks about? It seems to have all the necessary characteristics, including "humming sounds" that Bergier has noticed in other places.

Humming sounds of the sort that might be associated with high voltage utility lines are common in places that my associates and I have researched where the unusual light-forms manifest. Such sounds are present at Bragg Road, in the Mexican desert where we first saw the MPD effect in the mountains, in the Chinati Mountains near the site of the Marfa Light, and at Enchanted Rock. Indeed, Enchanted Rock probably got its name from Indians hearing such a sound emanating from it. A peculiar thing about these sounds is that they are not always present and not everyone can hear them. In our case my associates and I have all been able to hear the sounds at the same time at any given location.

There has been substantial media coverage within the last few years of a similar phenomenon in New Mexico called the Taos Hum. This sound, which is pervasive and covers a large area near Taos, has driven some people to distraction and others to speculate whether there might be some kind of underground secret government experimental installation in the area. Still others have not even been able to hear the hum at all. John Keel points out that such sounds are heard almost continuously in many places around the world including parts of Yellowstone Park and the Pascagoula River in Mississippi, which is known as "the singing river" because of the persistent sounds.

Sounds like lawn mowers or small engines running continuously throughout the night are also heard in these places. Researchers of both ghost light and mystery humanoid sightings areas have variously described mysterious sounds as "the odd, high-pitched tuning-fork sound....," or as "a high-pitched whining noise that...seemed to trail off at a distance," or as a sound like, "a logging truck pulling up a hill it never reaches the top of."

These descriptions are more accurate than you might think. The truck sound describes exactly what Stan and I heard one night just after dusk near Enchanted Rock in Llano County. We were at the old serpentine mine on Willow City Loop, gathering serpentine to take with us on a visit to La Quemada, the sacred mountain of the Huicholes Indians in Mexico, when we first heard it. We thought a large truck was approaching. The mine is on an elevated area, from which we could see a good distance down the road in both directions. Even though the sound was getting louder and louder, there was no truck in sight. Eventually the sound was right upon us and seemed to be coming from above before it began fading away. Though the night was clear and we had an unobstructed view in every direction, we never saw a truck, airplane, helicopter, or anything that could account for the sound.

One night while camping in the Rosier Unit of the Big Thicket Preserve Bill and I heard what sounded like the droning sound of small engines in the distance. It seemed odd at the time because it was well after midnight, and we were at least two miles through dense woods from the nearest human habitation. At this same location on an earlier trip, Stan and I saw a single pinpoint light in the treetops. It was identical to the one that Bill and I had witnessed on Bragg Road.

There was another curious incident that occurred at this site that provides further evidence of unusual magnetic conditions. I once spotted a male Western Tanager there during the spring migrations. From many years spent learning to identify the bird species native to the Big Thicket, I knew this was a very rare sighting. It was an absolutely positive identification. This is a bird with very bright contrasting colors and distinctive markings, and I was no more than twenty yards or so from it and using a pair of powerful binoculars.

What makes this sighting so unusual is that the Western Tanager normally comes no closer to the Big Thicket than far to the west in West Texas. Even in its normal range it prefers the high elevations of the mountains, yet here it was seven or eight hundred miles from what should be its natural migration route, right smack in the middle of a vast swampland, not more than fifty or sixty feet above sea level.

Something had that poor bird extremely confused. Birds are thought to use their sensitivity to the earth's magnetic field to guide them in their migrations. But how would that relate to the unusual magnetic conditions of that part of the Thicket? Could it have lost its way and then have been attracted by the energy in the Thicket, or could it have inadvertently taken a weird short-cut?

This bird could have gone from one location with unusual

magnetic conditions to another through a space unfamiliar to us. The appearance of out-of-place natural animals, such as wild kangaroos seen briefly in the U.S., are often cited in paranormal literature as possible examples of inadvertent teleportation through naturally occurring "worm-holes." This phenomenon may be more common than we think. And except in the case of obviously misplaced animals like kangaroos its effect might go unnoticed. If I hadn't happened to have been in that particular place where the Western Tanager showed up, and if I didn't happen to know that it shouldn't have been there, and if I didn't know about the unusual magnetic conditions that long have manifested in this area, it is likely that no one would have noticed this incident.

Bergier wrote that with the help of Einstein, the American physicist John Wheeler conceived of "topological wormholes," which are "trajectories in the refined atmospheric structure that allow passage from one point in space to another, without once crossing over into ordinary space." These wormholes have to do with the curvature of space affected by intense energy, and he cites Wheeler's theory to support the possibility of secret doors.

Of course, it is usually assumed that wormholes would only connect vastly distant points of space on a macrocosmic or galactic level and would not occur on a level that would be subject to human experience. But Bergier believes otherwise. He refers to another aspect of Wheeler's work to suggest that the same physical principles involved in wormholes can be used to actually create secret doors within the earth by utilizing what Wheeler calls "geometrodynamic energy." These immense energies, "greater than those generated by the annihilation of matter, are to be found in the structure of space itself."

Bergier points out that it is consistent with the theory of relativity that natural forces that modify space do exist, and that space is modified, "by both the magnetic field and the electric field," of which Wheeler's geometrodynamic energy may be the source. Because of this he speculates that, "the special curve which separates the various earths," (or Riemann surfaces) from each other, "can in turn be modified and that we can thereby create doors on earth which will also lead to aspects of the world not usually perceived." Whereas wormholes may be naturally occurring, Bergier makes it clear that he thinks the secret doors are actually created by conscious entities and that in the process of creating the doors, "psychic energy can act as a catalyst to Wheeler's geometrodynamic energy."

The energy necessary for a door to be opened may then occur when the massive magnetic intensities we have observed and documented in the Big Thicket and other wild places are active. The necessary psychic component of the creation of the doors Bergier postulates may be in evidence in the enigmatic appearances and disappearances of the wild man, the Karankawas, and in the Cajun legends of shape-shifting voodoo practitioners. These are beings who apparently know how to manipulate the energy psychically to access spaces that would be invisible to us.

Even though we may not be as aware of these energies as other beings, since we are also conscious beings, theoretically we should be affected by these same psychic and geometrodynamic energy fields, indicated by the ghost lights' presence. The difference between us and these other beings may be that our worldview conditions us to believe, and therefore experience, consciousness only locally, with our brains or bodies and their immediate surroundings. If, as is implied by the ghost lights, there can be consciousness not associated with a physical body, perhaps other beings can experience consciousness non-locally as an ambient field. The reality of such a being, and the limitations of time and space upon it, would obviously be quite different from that of those limited to local consciousness.

Maverick philosopher Robert Anton Wilson knows of the existence of the ghost lights and what they imply about the field-effect of consciousness. In discussing the nature of consciousness in *The New Inquisition*, he wrote, "Consciousness, in this model, is not 'in' our heads. Our brains are merely local receivers; consciousness 'is' an aspect of the non-local field." All of us, he writes, "have strict imprinted and conditioned programs about what is 'real' and what is 'unreal'." These programs, which are largely determined by our cultural worldview, dictate what is "tuned in" from the non-local field as "reality." This tuning in is essentially an unconscious psychic act that we all perform continuously.

A creature more conscious of the tuning-in process and the non-local psychic energy field may not only be able to create secret doors and enter other realities through psychic manipulation of the energy present in the structure of space; it may also be able to enter our minds and either render itself invisible to us or affect how and what we perceive by manipulating what we tune in from the non-local field.

If the sounds we discussed earlier are associated with energy present in the structure of space and with naturally occurring wormholes, then we may better understand why the sounds seem to come from the beneath the surface of the earth. Researchers Ann Slate and Alan Berry reported a sound in a Bigfoot sighting area that "seemed to come from the bowels of the earth." This may explain why some researchers think the Sasquatch lives in underground caves or abandoned mines and why the wild man in the Big Thicket is frequently seen near sludge pits in the old oil fields. These represent penetrations of the earth's surface that reach into its depths. The notion that such beings may come from the structure of space itself may be too bizarre for our conscious minds to comprehend, so the content of the tuning-in process of our deep psyches allows us to see them as coming from within the earth.

There may be some relation here to the hollow earth theory. The ancient notion that we live on a hollow earth is easy to dismiss if we take it to mean the naïve belief that, as Mike Dash describes in *Borderlands*, the earth, "is extensively honeycombed with giant caverns and cave systems and inhabited by the dead, or perhaps, by not entirely human beings."

As Dash points out, this belief has been revived in various forms by such writers as John Cleves Symmes, Ray Palmer, and Raymond Bernard, including the idea, "that some apparently paranormal creatures, such as Bigfoot, are really dwellers in a hollow earth." Dash believes that the theory has "attracted much greater attention than is warranted by the evidence."

But the evidence is considerably more compelling if we understand that the notion of a hollow earth might be an interpretation of phenomena resulting from energies within the structure of space, or from the Riemann surfaces or the layers of three dimensional space mentioned by Bergier. The transient appearance of mystery creatures associated with the hollow earth theory may, at the very least, suggest that three dimensional space is more complex than is normally imagined.

Whether they are related to the structure of space or to the subterranean depths, it may be that we are manipulated to envision these creatures as wild, hairy and ape-like. Their real form, in their non-localized state of consciousness, however, may more resemble balls of light.

In previous chapters I warned the reader of the inherent dangers of pursuing the wild man and the Karankawas. John Keel warned his readers that insanity, mysterious deaths, and suicide are not uncommon among serious paranormal investigators. It could be that their brains were adversely affected by exposure to unusual energies. But it could also be that their minds were intentionally and malevolently scrambled.

Russian peasants outside St. Petersburg believe that encounters with the wild man creatures seen in the forests for hundreds of years can have serious consequences. Like the Native American belief in the Sasquatch, they believe the wild man has extraordinary psychic powers, and that even chance encounters with it can result in mysterious illness, madness, or death. Speaking from my own experience with a peculiar and vicious malady, I came down with shortly after a series of puzzling experiences in the Big Thicket, I would advise anyone to not take these warnings lightly.

For some time I believed that the energy that manifests as the ghost light on Bragg Road actually has its source elsewhere in the Thicket. Bill and I arranged a short expedition with three of our friends to survey a particular area in the Preserve south of Bragg Road. We arrived separately in different stages. I left Bill to set up camp at the old bridge in the Preserve near the site of numerous wild man sightings, and set out to Bragg Road to meet Chip Yantis and Stan, who were driving in from Austin, and Jake Boaz, who was joining us from nearby Lumberton.

After a couple of uneventful hours on the Ghost Road, we all joined Bill back at the bridge to finish setting up camp. As soon as we arrived, Bill informed us that just after I had left, about thirty minutes after dusk, he heard what could have been the characteristic howling of the wild man on the edge of a marsh not more than fifty yards or so from our campsite. There was no mistaking that it was something unusual, he said, it was loud and had a deep, reverberating resonance. This obviously put us all in a vigilant mood, but the night passed without further incident or sign of the wild man's presence.

The next morning we explored the area just north of the

bridge and early that afternoon we drove to a nearby trail head a few miles away. The five of us planned to spread out on either side of the trail about twenty yards apart in the thick woods, in order to cover as much ground as possible, and proceed south for about two miles toward where the bayou intersects a pipeline. Before we could get started, Stan and Jake, for different personal reasons, were forced to cut short their adventures and return home. That left Bill, Chip, and me to carry on.

We had gone about a half mile when our path was blocked by a mother razorback sow with a litter of half-grown piglets. They were obviously wary of us, but they seemed panicked, and would not simply retreat in the direction from which they had come. It was as if they were running from something behind them which they considered a greater threat than us. After waiting on the high side of the bayou above a stand of bald cypresses for the wild hogs to leave, we began to notice something unusual in our perceptual fields.

It was as if in the periphery of our vision we could see shadows of varying sizes against the wall of trees or the forest floor, but when we turned to look, the shadows disappeared and there was nothing to cast the shadows we saw. If we had been alone, we probably would have dismissed this sensation, but we all experienced it separately before we began to talk about it, and it did seem unusual.

Chip and I both noticed a sudden change come over Bill. He seemed tired or suddenly not well. Chip asked him how he was feeling. "This is deep," Bill said, with a certain tone in his voice and a look in his eyes that told me he was picking up on something. Bill is sensitive in these situations, so I was not surprised to see Bill and Chip sit there meditatively awhile before returning to camp. For some reason, however, I decided to stay out a little longer and go further down the bayou alone.

I stopped to sit with my back against a large beech tree and tried to clear my mind. Whether my imagination was fueled by the strange visual sensations we had already experienced, or by Bill's observation, I honestly don't know, but I began to have an odd audible sensation. I could hear sounds like footsteps, muffled by the thick layer of leaves on the forest floor, but occasionally accented by the loud snap of twigs and sticks being broken, as if something were sneaking up on me from behind. When I would turn to look, the sounds would stop and nothing was there.

When I got up to walk farther down the bayou I began to hear what sounded like the barely muffled din of a large group of people engaged in lively conversation. I could not make out what anyone was saying. But at one point, as unlikely as it seemed for being so far out in the woods, I fully expected to come across a party of some kind just around the next bend in the bayou, but when I would go a little farther, the sound would stop or would seem just slightly farther away. It was the audible equivalent of a mirage, and it reminded me of how the ghost lights are said to sometimes recede from observers who attempt to approach them.

Bill and I had both heard something similar along Legion Creek in Llano County one time when we were hiking to Cedar Mountain. It reminded me of the old Celtic tradition that associates such sounds with the presence of mischief-making fairies and warns that hearing them can lead to madness. Feeling unnerved, I decided to join Bill and Chip, and got back to camp just as it was turning dark.

Later that night we all went to a pipeline right-of-way that cuts through the woods near our campsite. We took lawn chairs and sat for hours taking advantage of the open skies and distant perspectives provided by the pipeline. We had brought binoculars and my camera in case we saw anything interesting. It was in the late spring and the fireflies were out in abundance. We tried without success to photograph them to compare them to the pinpoint lights that we had photographed earlier.

The ghost light didn't show up, nor did the pinpoint lights, but we did see another type of light-form we could not identify and which we had at first confused with the fireflies. There were dozens of tiny lights in every direction flashing on and off like the fireflies, but they were red and smaller than firefly lights, and they seemed more intensely bright and sharply defined. Unlike the fireflies, which would come to within arm's length and even light on us, the red lights remained more distant. We could all see them, and it was obvious that they were not caused by insects. They also didn't show up on film when we tried to photograph them. We could only guess that they were yet another luminous manifestation of the Big Thicket's mysterious energy fields, and we wondered whether they were related to our earlier visual experiences with the shadows.

Within days of our return to Austin I began to suffer from a mild depression. Before I knew it, it got progressively worse. Within a couple of weeks I was overcome with a sense of utter despair and hopelessness, and I became increasingly weak and listless. I could not understand where such intense emotions were coming from. Nothing like this had ever happened to me before, (and thankfully not since). I even entertained suicidal thoughts, but I also struggled against them, as if they were not my own thoughts. Luckily, I remembered Keel's observation and went to Farrell Brenner, a friend and licensed mental health professional and certified counselor.

I knew Farrell was knowledgeable about the effect of electromagnetic fields, both man-made and naturally occurring, on psychological and physical well being. I told him the details of our recent trip to the Thicket, which I began to suspect were involved with my illness. Farrell listened to the story with interest and with the genuine concern of an old friend. We arranged to meet the next day at a local restaurant where we frequently dined to discussing our respective research. He gave me a small glass bottle, about the size of my pinky finger, that contained a clear liquid he had prepared in a manner similar to a homeopathic remedy. I was to put a few drops on my tongue three times a day, he said, and I was to keep the bottle with me at all times. Within a few days I returned to normal.

Farrell said he had heard of similar cases and thought it likely that I had suffered from a psychic infection, caused by a pollution or contamination of the energy I had encountered, or perhaps by negative events that had transpired in that same space. This had created an imbalance which resulted in mental distress that rapidly progressed toward physical disease. He also conceded, as I suspected, that I could have been subjected to some kind of psychic attack by another entity. So the Russian peasants around St. Petersburg may be right. The wild man may have powers in his self-defense arsenal that we can scarcely imagine.

No matter how bizarre the notion of psychically activated worm-holes and doors opening on to other worlds may seem to us now, Bergier predicts that "The physicist may someday be as familiar with this idea as he is with infrared or ultraviolet photography." These, of course, are frequencies of light that lie outside the spectrum visible to ordinary human perception. Bergier speculates that there may be entire realities that would be accessible to us by artificial means just as we have learned to utilize the infrared and ultraviolet bands to be able to photograph what we cannot see with the unaided eye. Similar ideas have been advanced by John A. Keel.

Whereas Bergier speaks of doors created by immense concentrations of energy, Keel writes of what he calls "window areas." All living things appear to radiate energy in the same portion of the electromagnetic spectrum as the energy radiated by the Earth the Sun, the stars, and other celestial bodies. Keel observes that "...there is a constant exchange of this energy between organisms, and the organisms are influenced by energy waves from many sources on many frequencies." The ebb and flow of the natural magnetic field of the earth exerts an influence on the biological energy within organisms just as it may affect the weather, Keel maintains. The pulse of the Earth's field is, no doubt, involved in and affected by an energy exchange of cosmic proportions, but it is most obviously affected, as Keel points out, by the sun's magnetic field and especially by solar magnetic storms.

When these disturbances occur, magnetic deviations are widespread but seem to focus in particular areas. As Keel has pointed out, it is in these areas, which may also be related to highly localized power outages, that the range of paranormal phenomena including UFO, mystery light, and mystery creature sightings, most commonly occurs.

Keel calls such places "window areas," a term reminiscent of the ancient Celtic belief in the existence of places where the boundary between this and other worlds sometimes grows thin. He does not consider the phenomena that occur in such places to be hallucinatory, rather he considers them to be actual intrusions from other realities into this space-time continuum. Our senses are equipped to pick up only a small range of the known electromagnetic spectrum, those frequencies included in visible light and audible sound. That range within our sensory capacity constitutes reality to us; what we experience as space and time occur within that continuum. Keel thinks that there may be entire worlds that lie outside the normal reach of our senses, denizens of which may temporarily be perceivable during a paranormal episode.

Three hypotheses may help explain how such intrusions occur. The first is that the energies involved literally rend the fabric of space-time in a highly localized area. In this case the window is opened, and like cat burglars in the night, certain beings can pass back and forth between this and other dimensions through the window. The mechanism would probably involve a psychic component. The Native American view of the activities of Bigfoot corresponds closely to this theory.

The second possibility is that exposure to this energy temporarily enhances perception, allowing some people to see or hear (or tune in, to use Wilson's term) what is normally outside the range of the senses. There is an analogy to this notion of a "window" in electronics. Normally we think that magnetic storms or unusual magnetic conditions disrupt radio transmissions. But in some cases, exposure to a strong electromagnetic field can extend the range of radio reception. This phenomenon was reported to the *Beaumont Enterprise* reporter who covered the Beaumont blackout that I discussed previously. I have also noticed this on a number of other occasions in the same region. It may be that some people are being affected similarly, enabling them to see such things as the wild man.

Strong magnetic anomalies can also produce a bleed-over effect in radio reception. Under these conditions it may be that aspects of realities at one frequency may temporarily bleed into another, again making visible that which would otherwise not be visible. If this is true of spatial dimensions, could it also affect the dimension of time?

Another theory, the "time-lines" theory, holds that the past does not simply disappear, but still exists on another time-line. If there are time-line bleeds corresponding to radio frequency bleeds caused by immense electromagnetic anomalies, it is conceivable that appearances of the mystery creatures and

Karankawas may be as much from another time-line as from another spatial dimension.

A third speculation is that the strange things witnessed during a paranormal event are externalized projections of the minds of the perceivers. At first glance this would amount to saying that exposure to the energy simply causes the mind to hallucinate or to project internally stored images that are consistent with cultural reality and personal experience. In this theory, the wild man, the black panthers, and the ghost lights, strange as they are, are no more than exotic secretions of the mind.

This is Persinger's position, and he makes a convincing case for it. The temporal lobes of the brain, he says, are involved in the formation of "external reality." When they are stimulated by electromagnetic energy, the mind will experience hallucinations that even people who enjoy normal mental health cannot distinguish from reality. What makes Persinger's case so compelling, as Dennis Stacy makes clear in an article in the December 1988 issue of *Omni* magazine, is that Persinger has been able to duplicate this effect under controlled laboratory conditions with a helmet that produces mild electromagnetic stimulation in the brains of test subjects who then report paranormal-like experiences. It is exposure to such energy from natural sources, Persinger believes, that accounts for wild man, Sasquatch, and black panther sightings.

To those who want to hold on to a materialistic model of reality, this theory may be the most comfortable of the three, but it does have problems. If these sightings are purely hallucinatory, why do so many witnesses have virtually identical sightings? Why would so many report seeing ape-like creatures? Why not something else? The theory also fails to take into account the tangible evidence left behind, such as foot prints and claw marks. Clearly, there is more objectivity and consistency to these sightings than would be expected if they were merely hallucinatory. As intriguing as Persinger's lab work is, it does little more than demonstrate how the brain's mechanism of perception responds to artificial stimulation. It could be argued that the temporal lobes are always responding to electromagnetic stimuli during the normal process of perception.

The temporal lobes may function similarly in both electromagnetically induced hallucinations and in normal perception, and it is only the degree of objectivity that normally allows us to determine whether something is real or imaginary. If I have an hallucination of a speeding Mack truck, it's not going to run me over, but an objective Mack truck that I and others can perceive has the capacity to run me over, even though my mind might not have been able to distinguish between the hallucination and the reality. Moreover, it may be that all perceptions are subjective and hallucinatory; perhaps the conditioning involved in the tuning in process allows us to perceive an object as objectively real. The objective reality of the wild man may be closer to that of the real Mack truck than to the hallucinatory truck or to any electromagnetically induced hallucination of a wild man.

Unusual electromagnetic conditions may short-circuit the process that usually tunes out the perception of such things as the wild man. If exposure to unusual energies temporarily enhances the perceptual range of the senses and enables some people to see what is not normally perceptible, the temporal lobes may be electrically stimulated just as in Persinger's experiments. It would only be the evidence for objectivity–the presence of multiple witnesses or physical traces–that could distinguish such a perception from hallucination.

Many of the witnesses of the Big Thicket's wild man are totally shocked and surprised at what they see, and they are also usually ignorant of the fact that such creatures are seen by others in the same area. It is unlikely, then, that the perceived contents of their sightings were influenced from established folklore or stories they had heard. It is also unlikely that the minds of the witnesses share any expectations about the existence of ape-like creatures in the Thicket so that exposure to magnetic anomalies would stimulate their brains in such a way that their expectations would be projected externally.

That said, wild man stories do arise from time to time in various places in the Thicket. The stories tend, however, to be highly localized, as in the cases of Ol' Mossyback and the Raggedy Man, with no consistent image of the wild man's appearance or nature. Only rarely are such stories given media treatment, and when they do the stories usually end up being dismissed or attributed to such mundane things as escaped convicts or fanciful misperceptions by gullible witnesses. Even these stories are not normally widely circulated.

A good case in point is an article by John Jefferson that appeared in the October 2000 issue of *Texas Parks & Wildlife* magazine, which recounts the stories of the Caney Head Wildman told by Tanner Hunt, a Beaumont lawyer. "Hunt recalls that the man was seen several times in automobile headlights on backwoods roads. He was always naked, barefoot, had hair to his waist–and disappeared. Other stories placed alleged 'wildmen' in other parts of the Thicket. Living naked amid mosquito-infested swamps made the creature supernatural in the minds of the locals. Any time an animal was mysteriously killed or disappeared, the wild man was listed among the usual suspects."

Other than my own stories in the *Kountze News* in 1979, this was, to my knowledge, the first printed reference to the Big Thicket wild man since Abernethy's 1966 book, *Tales from the Big Thicket*. But Jefferson concludes that the Big Thicket wild man is no more than the product of the imagination. He calls the

Thicket, and the strange stories coming from its depths, a place, "where legend is often more compelling than fact."

The transient nature of the creatures cannot be denied. I must admit that the creatures are apparently not a real part of this world in a normal sense of the word. If we discount Bergier's theory of wormholes and secret doors to account for the wild man's appearances and disappearances, and if this means that he is in some way hallucinatory, then how do we account for the fact that confrontations are interpreted basically the same way by the minds of so many different witnesses?

Researchers Clarke, Devereux, and Philip Heselton have suggested that the energy associated with ghost light and mystery creature sightings is extremely sensitive to consciousness. "The energy which creates earth lights," Heselton observes, "seems to have a sensitizing effect on people so that they are more likely to see things psychically." This is similar to the expanded perception range theory, discussed previously but with a subtle difference. Heselton believes that when subjected to such energies the projections of the minds of observers are not purely hallucinatory, despite the transience or impermanence of the creatures and objects seen. Rather, he says, "the energy plasma appears to be sensitive to psychic and thought forms, so that it can actually move or change shape according to the mind of the observer."

In other words, although the energy may respond to the minds of observers, it is an act of the energy itself that determines what shape it presents to the observer. This is similar to Keel's idea that the progression of phases of different lights and creatures that we have discussed represents transformations of the same base energy in response to the minds of the observers. If witnesses are "hallucinating," it is the energy which consciously and deliberately causes the hallucinations. It is not sub-conscious self-delusion by the witnesses.

There is a principle of scientific investigation that enjoins us to always seek the simplest explanation for any given phenomenon without resorting to false unknowns or unnecessarily complicated schemes that ignore the obvious facts. The most commonly cited theories that seek to account for the rare phenomena detailed in this book have been presented. You have seen that not only is the origin and nature of the ghost lights a genuine mystery, but they are also apparently causally related to the equally mysterious appearances of the wild man. Given all that has been considered, what would be the simplest explanation for the phenomena without simply ignoring their existence or dismissing them outright?

I tend to agree with Keel and Heselton that the energy itself is responding to the minds of its observers. That's one way of saying that the ghost lights act like conscious entities. Much of what I have presented here is little more than a concession to the mental gymnastics that most of us have to go through to even remotely consider what would be blatantly obvious to any Native American shaman, and what was so disturbingly self-evident to my friend Jim: "That damn light was alive!"

The late Ted Holiday would not disagree. In *The Goblin Universe,* Holiday's classic study of recurrent paranormal phenomena in Great Britain, he concludes that ghost lights, UFOs, and mystery creature sightings relate to the fairy folklore of the ancient Celtic people of Western Europe. Holiday specifically refers to "the wandering Sighes or Trooping Fairies," who he says were known for their "illusions and paranormal hoaxes." In relating them to UFO reports, he wrote: "The fairies were said to travel through the air in troops or waves at periodic intervals; UFOs do the same." Fairies appear to humans like radiantly beautiful light, and when they gather in large groups to go about their mischief making, they supposedly resemble large balls of light that in modern times would be taken for UFOs.

In agreement with Keel's window area theory, Holiday notes that both UFOs and the Trooping Fairies are associated with places that exhibit recurrent spikes in the local magnetic field; there are also cycles that correspond to both phenomena. "Since the magnetic storms on the sun, known as sunspots, fluctuate through an 11 year cycle and are the biggest single cause of variations in the earth's magnetic field, it appears that UFOs are cyclic in character, just as folklore observed." He further states that the Trooping Fairies were called Earth Gods, "possibly because they use the earth's magnetic flux in order to manifest."

The strange humming sounds frequently heard in ghost light and wild man sightings areas, which Bergier associated with secret doors, also have their counterpart in Celtic fairy lore. When the amassed group of Trooping Fairies alights or takes off, they were said to sound like a loud swarm of bees. Scandinavian folklore holds that fairies live underground within mounds, which again ties in to the idea of sounds coming from deep within the earth. Holiday concludes that these are not mere resemblances but that the fairy and UFO phenomena are identical, the only difference being that the UFO phenomenon "has simply acquired a technical facade to suit the expectations of modern observers."

The range of paranormal phenomena exhibited cyclically in the Big Thicket would not surprise Holiday. The large, orange fireballs fit the description of the amassed fairy troops; that one was seen near a place called Big Hill on several occasions even suggests that the Southeast Texas fairies may have their own mound to call home. It makes you wonder if they speak with a drawl. The wild man appearances, the ghost lights, the pin-point lights, and the black panthers are all typical manifestations of the prankster fairies. Holiday would also not be surprised to hear of the old man who went crazy trying to find the strange object he saw in the woods on the bayou south of Sour Lake, or of my bout of sickness after my weird experiences in the Thicket. Holiday notes that over the last 20 years such things "have left behind an impressive catalogue of suicides, psychiatric cases and shocked individuals."

But to call the beings behind these manifestations fairies is no more accurate than to call them the wild man or ghost lights. The fairy form simply suited the expectations of observers from earlier times. Holiday, like Keel, views this as a "reflective phenomenon," and that, "Chameleonlike, they can switch their format to suit the observer's preconceptions, only to leave him staring glassy-eyed at nothing."

The conclusions of Holiday and Keel are compelling and seem to fit the patterns of the Big Thicket phenomena. There is one other model of explanation, however, that must be considered, and it may prove to be an even simpler explanation. I hinted at it earlier in the discussion of the Cajun shape-shifter legends of the fifolet, or ghost light, and the loup garoux, the South Louisiana equivalent of the neighboring Big Thicket wild man. Rather than being denizens of other worlds, the source of the phenomena, in these two adjacent areas at least, may be human beings. These humans are not deluded and hallucinating, however; they are people who have developed extraordinary powers. There could be voodoo on the bayou–on both sides of the Sabine River.

Remember the story of the wizard, Medeo, who lived deep in the Atchafalaya swamp and was said to be able to transform himself into the fifolet at will? This legend almost certainly has its roots in voodoo tradition. If all you know about voodoo is the casting of evil spells by sticking pins in dolls, and you think such spells work only because the superstitious believe that they do, you probably think stories of wizards like Medeo are equally superstitious.

The voodoo tradition of South Louisiana has its source in

Africa and spread via Haiti. In voodoo, as practiced in Haiti, it is obvious that we are dealing with objective manifestations of psychically directed unusual energies and strange powers of the mind similar to those associated with the phenomena in this work. One of the best such studies is by the Belgian author, explorer, and filmmaker, Douchan Gersi.

Gersi spent his childhood and part of his adolescence with his family deep in the Belgian Congo where they had fled as political refugees from Czechoslovakia. There he was exposed to magicians, shamans and sorcerers on a daily basis. Gersi said he "lived according to realities different from those of our modern world," and "witnessed amazing and inexplicable things." One of his most vivid experiences involved a ceremony performed by a powerful sorcerer named Moduku; its intention was to kill an enemy who had harmed Moduku.

Moduku's house was filled with dark smoke from a small campfire. While performing incantations, he filled a calabash with feathers and blood from a black chicken he had sacrificed. When he lit the contents of the calabash, heavy smoke poured forth as Moduku began chanting unintelligibly. Gersi wrote, "Slowly the smoke became very strange. Colors began to form bizarre faces—not human faces, nor those of animals or birds, but faces nonetheless." Eventually Gersi was frightened and ran back to his parents' home. "And after long sleepless hours, I had a series of nightmares in which the strange faces I had seen in the smoke appeared."

The next day Gersi discovered that Moduku had disappeared and his enemy had met with a strange and sudden death. The man was discovered "dead, stone-cold dead, and yet standing on his feet, leaning against the wall of his hut. Between his fingers were the ashes of a cigarette that had continued to burn after he died." Gersi's father concluded that only lightning could have killed a man so suddenly and left him standing. "But since there had been no thunder that night, my father said, the man must have been struck by a magic death."

After Gersi's father died, the family moved back to Belgium, where he entered college, and "tried to live according to the modern world's reality." There he says he struggled with "the constrictions of rationalism," and found himself doubting his own memory of the wonders he had witnessed in the Congo. From this conflict Gersi dedicated the remainder of his life to finding out if what he had "learned, heard, and seen" as a child in Africa was real, "and, if it was real, to what reality it belonged."

"I wanted to know if I would see faces in the smoke elsewhere—and I did," wrote Gersi. "I found them while studying Voodoo in Haiti for five years. I found them among the Tuareg of the Sahara Desert and the shamans of the Andes. In fact, among almost all people who live according to realities other than ours, I have been able, in one way or another, to see faces in the smoke."

Gersi's account resembles our earlier report on the two faces in the smoke. It seems likely that the face of the ancient Indian seen in the smoke of the forest fire was another example of spirit manifestations conjured up by people with extraordinary powers who live in a reality quite foreign to modern Western culture. Could the wild man face in the smoke-like glowing mist on Bragg Road be connected with some kind of magic practice? It's an intriguing possibility, especially given the Big Thicket wild man's similarity to the Cajun voodoo-influenced legend of the shapeshifting loup garoux, and the fact that the voodoo practices that spread to Louisiana from Haiti were also practiced in Southeast Texas in the Galveston area.

Earlier in this chapter I discussed how our culturally determined worldview prevents our perception of realities that lie outside the reach of the senses, or limits our ability to tune in these realities from the non-local psychic field. I also explained how exposure to unusual magnetic energy fields can sometimes bypass the tuning-in mechanism, increasing the psychic sensitivity of an observer, and thereby allowing the perception of normally unseen realities. From what Gersi has observed, it seems also possible for extraordinary human beings to access and direct the same mysterious energy fields, for psychic purposes but with objective, physical results.

To do this you must hold to a worldview quite different from the rationality and philosophical materialism typical of modern industrialized societies. Gersi claims to have witnessed many mysterious powers, which he thinks may be remnants of abilities once possessed by all mankind, "whether to contact forces outside of us or to make use of powers (psychic and otherwise) that are still within us." He finds that such powers are more common culture-wide among those he calls "people of tradition."

With this term he refers to "all peoples who live following age-old traditions instead of moving with the flow of the twentieth century." These are people with tribal structure and/or shamanic practices as the basis of their cultures. He says they may be part of the Third World or developing countries, or of Fourth World societies that remain outside the influence of modern culture.

Because of their different worldview, these people may seem to us backward, ignorant, superstitious, or unintelligent. Gersi thinks these people rely less on the parts of the brain involved in the thinking process and more on the parts of the brain that deal with altered states of consciousness. This makes them "in tune with a knowledge that, as some scientific research suggests, is carried in our mind-body systems–in our genetic memory. In this way they gain access to powers that we use only rarely and don't truly understand with our civilized conscious minds." If this sounds too speculative, consider again Gersi's adventures in Haiti.

The connection between the Big Thicket paranormal phenomena and voodoo or similar shamanic magic practice becomes ever more apparent.

The electromagnetic parameters of the Big Thicket phenomena, as we have noted, gives them their objectivity. No matter how we might account for what people witness in specific terms, the fact that there are physical effects means that something is happening that is more than imaginary. These effects usually take the form of electrical disturbances, including unusual radio and television reception, as well as automobile and power black-outs.

Gersi witnessed many similar electrical effects during his observation of voodoo phenomena. Gersi is a professional photographer with years of experience operating photographic equipment. On several occasions he attempted to photograph the levitations he witnessed during voodoo ceremonies involving spirit possession. From experience he became convinced that there was no fraud or trickery involved in these levitations, but he was never able to successfully photograph the phenomenon.

Each time something interfered with his ability to record the incident. Frequently the batteries that powered his movie camera would die just as the levitation began. Even the batteries of the lighting system, the tape recorder, and his watch battery "would all give up just at the time someone began levitating."

If this had happened only once, it might be considered coincidental. But Gersi claims it happened more than twenty times, all with separate sets of batteries. He speculates that "the state of levitation–that is, the manipulation of gravitational forces and perhaps forces related to other principles of physics–itself develops such a quantity of energy that it short-circuits all batteries, killing them instantly."

Curiously, on two occasions Gersi's batteries did not die when filming a levitation. But in these instances the frames that corresponded with the exact time of the levitations would be so dark and out of focus that it was impossible to tell what was going on, even though the adjacent frames would be clear, sharp and in focus. Still photography produced the same results. These repeated failures imply intent; it is as if the energy was not just present, but also consciously directed. It reminds me of Bill's intuitive observation that we did not obtain the photographs of the pinpoint lights and the glowing mist without some kind of willfulness on the part of the lights—as if they had allowed themselves to be photographed.

The possible voodoo connection with the Big Thicket phenomena is even more apparent in Gersi's study of "the Flying Men." This Haitian society has many lodges all over the island. Its members may or may not also practice voodoo, but are very secretive about belonging to the sect. Gersi claims that some are capable of de-materializing in one place and re-materializing somewhere else. He claims to have witnessed this on several occasions.

Eventually Gersi was befriended by Saint-Germain, the head of the Flying Men lodges in Haiti. Saint-Germain was more than willing to share his knowledge of the techniques involved and performed the feat several times for Gersi, each time disappearing in plain view and then reappearing. He gave Gersi permission to photograph the episodes, but again in each case, his movie equipment failed.

Of course, even if Gersi had been able to film these events, he could always be accused of having faked the photographs, especially since video computer special effects are so easy to produce these days. Gersi was also concerned that he was somehow being deceived, so he asked his friend if he could put him to the test. He asked Saint-Germain to fly to the room in his friend Jean's house where Gersi was staying in Port-au-Prince, about a hundred miles away, and pick up anything he could find that he could bring back as proof that he had been there.

After giving him directions to Jean's house, Gersi watched Saint-Germain disappear suddenly, dematerializing completely. "Exactly thirty-two minutes after he had disappeared," Gersi wrote, "Saint-Germain reappeared. He materialized next to the bed, holding a small notebook in which I used to write notes about my sound tapes after listening to them–a notebook that I never took along when I left Port-au-Prince, because I was scared of losing it."

These disappearances and reappearances, of course, sound very much like stories of the wild man. The Flying Men appear to have psychic abilities similar to those of the legendary ape-like creatures, those that have to do with the ability to consciously enter the non-local psychic energy field. There may be a connection to the ghost light, fifolet, shape-shifting legends as well.

Saint-Germain invited Gersi to attend an annual meeting in which all the members of the Flying Men lodges meet for one night at a different place each year. They are allowed to come only by flying. After waiting for two hours and watching the sky from the top of a temporary shelter erected for the event, Gersi wrote, "And then, all of a sudden, hundreds of small luminescent points appeared in the sky and beneath the clouds for a second or two, their mobility contrasting with the motionlessness of the stars." Before he knew it the meeting area was crowded with more than six or seven hundred people, and just beneath him, looking up with a big smile on his face, was Saint-Germain.

From Gersi's description, it seems the Flying Men transform themselves into points of light in order to be able to make their flights. If there is an entire secret society of people capable of such feats in Haiti, might there be a comparable people, perhaps smaller in numbers, in the Bayou Country and the Big Thicket whose similar activities may be seen as the ghost lights and pinpoint lights, and the face in the luminous smoke-like fog? Might there really be a few isolated old wizards like Medeo living in the swamp who actually can become the fifolet and go flying into the night? Do the legends of hermits and old Indians with magic powers living deep in the Thicket, and rumors of covens of witches meeting there in their secret places, protected from the outside world by miles of thick brush and clouds of mosquitoes, have a basis in fact?

I have already noted that the loup garoux or werewolf legends among the Cajuns might duplicate or overlap with the wild man stories. Gersi also uncovered evidence of werewolves in Haiti that could be linked to secret voodoo sects of shape-shifters, who can appraently transform themselves, not only into werewolves, but into other animal forms as well. Could one of these other animal forms be a black panther?

The case for a cultural connection between voodoo practice in Haiti and Louisiana and the Big Thicket's paranormal phenomena is certainly intriguing, but in some way it is even more fascinating to think that there might not be any cultural influence at all. The similarities may be due to a universality of certain magical practices that are rooted in the relationship between the human nervous system and the energies that are inherent in the very structure of space.

In that case, what you might have in the Bayou Country, and the Big Thicket, and elsewhere is evidence of the activities of relict populations of one or more ancient tribal peoples, perhaps even an earlier form of human, thought to have long been extinct. Though they appear to us to live at a Stone Age level, they have retained and refined certain psychic and mental powers that might once have been inherent in all human beings. That thesis is consistent with, and accounts for, much of the circumstances of both the wild man and Karankawa sighting stories, and it is precisely what Swan's Native American medicine men friends say of the Sasquatch's origin and nature.

It may be that these wild tribal people manage to survive in relatively unpopulated areas of North America by employing magic practices similar to voodoo to camouflage themselves. They are thus able to keep themselves somewhat concealed from the population at large, their very existence reduced to the stuff of legend, while they pursue an ancient way of life based on a world-view and reality that, while profoundly attuned with nature, is quite alien to modern life. These Ancient Ones may be attracted to specific locations not just due to their sparse human populations but for an element of wildness to which we have become unconscious–the presence of periodic unusual magnetic conditions that are essential to support their psychic environment and facilitate their magic.

So, is this then the simplest model, the least fantastic explanation of the weird events involving strange lights that recur in the Big Thicket and other wild places? Let us review the options, each briefly summarized.

The first model is really no option at all since it is to simply deny that the phenomena occur, or to maintain that they are easily explained away as mistaken interpretations of common natural events and objects. If you still think this after having read this far, please go to the blackboard and write 500 times: "I will pay attention." Clearly, the only way to hold this position is to be a hopeless skeptic, since the electromagnetic elements of the phenomena alone give them legitimacy.

Another opinion is that the phenomena are bizarre hallucinations induced by chance encounters with rare, but naturally occurring electromagnetic energy fields. While compelling to some degree, this model ignores such physical evidence as foot prints, claw marks, and detailed multiple witness sightings.

The first model that views the phenomena as genuine unknowns involves unusual energy fields temporarily expanding the perceptual range of witnesses exposed to them, thus allowing the perception of beings, objects, and realities that are not normally visible.

The model best represented by Keel's window area theory, which overlaps somewhat with the previous option, is that periodic spikes of the earth's magnetic field and of the energy present in the very structure of space itself, cause transient tears or warps in the space-time continuum, allowing access to this world by denizens of other realities.

Heselton's model, on the other hand, is that the energy which produces the lights is keenly sensitive to consciousness and that it consciously and willfully reflects the contents of the minds of its observers. Similarly, Holiday holds that the lights are themselves conscious entities, accounts of which can be traced to the fairy stories and similar lore of Celtic and other cultures. Brenner refers to such entities as "life-forms without skin."

That brings us to what I think is the simplest model that takes the phenomena seriously; that is, that the various lights and strange creatures are actually manifestations by human beings, whether practitioners of voodoo or similar shamanic magic, and perhaps of an ancient form of mankind, employing psychic faculties that most of us cannot comprehend.

It should be clear from this discussion that a case can be made for any of these models, except for the one that ignores the phenomena. Of course, these models may be both partly right and partly wrong, or they may all be happening.

CHAPTER 6

Seeing Things Differently

Now that you've had your guided tour through the Big Thicket, and you've been introduced to the variety of weird things and events that are witnessed there and in other wild places, maybe you find yourself wondering what the implications of the existence of big, hairy wild men, phantom black panthers, spectral lights and out-of-place primitive Indians would be. If all these things are actually seen by reliable witnesses, they constitute more than mere curiosities; as I hope to have demonstrated, they bring into question our most basic assumptions about the nature of reality. If this account has led you to such ponderous thoughts, then the mystery of the Thicket has been at least somewhat adequately conveyed. You have joined the ranks of John Wacasey, Buddy Moore, and Frances Abernethey. You have been touched by the Holy Ghost of which Archer Fullingim wrote, and you are now a Hardin County-style natural philosopher.

If, indeed, the spirit has moved you, by now you should recognize that at least some of the elements of the strange goings-on that have been described in our wild places are what can only be described as paranormal phenomena. That is, they lie outside the range of our normal experience and the common-sense understanding of how the Universe works. There also is a strange link with the minds of observers that has been noted, and it may be that the lights themselves are conscious entities that willfully and deliberately interact with humans according to their own purposes, which to us are unimaginable.

This does not mean that any of these phenomena or their sources are supernatural or matters of faith that we can choose to either believe in or not. There are objectively real parameters to the phenomena, and the base phenomenon–the ghost lights and the energy associated with them–has physical effects. What it does mean, though, is that to proceed further in this inquiry we have to put on our philosopher's caps.

The fact that these phenomena occur within our perceptual range means that we have some faculty that corresponds to their nature, but we have to go beyond the limitations that are imposed on reason and our imaginations by a naively materialistic world-view. The worldview that has dominated Western technological culture since the Industrial Revolution, and that is increasingly global in scope, has scientific materialism as its basis.

The essence of this worldview is eloquently described by Paul Laffoley, the self-described artist/alchemist from Boston. Scientific materialism, he says, defines reality as the interactions of mass and energy. Everything that can be experienced or described can be done within these terms. According to this world-view, the existence of consciousness and the mind are totally accountable for as products of biochemical processes. Western psychology and physiology continue to try to reduce conscious-ness to material models, despite the fact that, as pointed out by British philosopher Graham Martin, physicists themselves doubt the very existence of matter apart from consciousness. The idea of a psychic nature influencing mass or energy, and directly affecting the essential structure of the physical world, never arises.

As we have seen, however, there are several models of expla-nation for the range of ghost light related phenomena that suggest that consciousness is not confined to matter. The ghost lights defi-antly fly in the face of the materialistic worldview, which they contradict and by which they cannot be explained adequately.

In contrast to the reality imposed by the materialistic worldview, Laffoley talks of what he calls alchemy. Within its terms, reality can be described as the interactions of energy, mass, and consciousness. Rather than being an accidental by-product of mass and energy evolving in time through a mechanical process, consciousness is an equal component of reality. The implications of the observer-created universe theory of physics are integrated into this worldview, and matter, or mass and energy, do not have an existence separate from consciousness. Within these terms, space and time would not be absolutes and the existence of paranormal events and the psychic realm, in which the mind can directly affect the basic structure of the physical world, would be at least theoretically predictable.

As we have seen, a worldview is not just a set of attitudes, opinions, and beliefs; it determines what is physically possible, as well as what is mentally conceivable. If it does not include consciousness as equal to mass and energy, those whose reality is defined by such a worldview will not be able to perform the kinds of feats that Gersi witnessed in Haiti and Africa; and the types of phenomena that are witnessed in our wild places will either be dismissed outright or be thought of as paranormal.

The vast majority of the people of the modern world can neither perform nor understand the magical practices that are common among so-called primitive people. By psychic means these practices actually tap into and manipulate immense physical forces. Whether we have lost this ability because our worldview emphasizes the use of parts of our brain that do not have this capacity, as Gersi thinks, or because our worldview has resulted in our not being able to tune in these energies and the realities to which they pertain, as Wilson would have it, makes no difference. The result is the same. In the modern world we are trapped, so to speak, in a closed-system universe in which matter and energy, space and time, are absolutes, and we have lost awareness of an entire dimension of ourselves.

The point here is not that we should seek to levitate or dematerialize and rematerialize at will or to enter portals to other realities. The point is, rather, that by having created what is increasingly a global culture that does not recognize our inherent psychic nature we have created a world that is badly out of balance and that is full of individuals who are increasingly out of balance and out of touch both with themselves, one another, and nature. The effects of this state of imbalance manifest as the increasingly pressing problems that face the world today and that threaten environmental disaster and social collapse.

We all know what such problems are: the pollution of the air and water; the threat of global warming that portends potentially devastating climatic changes; the increase in mindless violence and widespread social strife; the alienation of our youth and the attendant drug abuse. Many of us sense that something is fundamentally wrong; that even though we may be well intentioned, too often our best efforts merely serve to exacerbate these problems. We may need a different way of looking at things to open up a vision of new possibilities.

When the ideas leading to this book were in their formative stages, I gave a lecture at a fund-raising dinner that was very graciously arranged by Jeanie Turk and Steve Doukas of Pinewood to enable me to present a paper at Swan's Spirit of Place symposium in California. After the talk, which was well attended, my mother's blue-haired little old lady friend approached me. "Honey," she said in her soft Texas twang, "I'm not sure what you're talking about, but I'm just glad somebody's doing something." That dear lady's kind remarks were inspiring, and since that time the subtlety and implications of this research have made it more and more apparent that, indeed, there is much that can be done.

Actually, Southeast Texans began to do something about it long ago. Their efforts of several decades were finally rewarded with the creation of the Big Thicket National Preserve some twenty-five years ago. Most of the people who came to that dinner did so because they wanted to know what was going to be said about the ghost light. The light on the Ghost Road is a genuine mystery that many of those people had experienced for themselves. No doubt, just as my grandfather had passed along his reverence for the mystery of the Big Thicket to me, many of my listeners had had similar tales passed down from one generation to another within their own families. If the truth be known, the need to preserve the Big Thicket came as much from the subtle appreciation of a way of life that included a magical connection to Nature as from other environmental concerns.

We need to develop an ecological awareness that includes preserving the places where the types of phenomena we have discussed take place, the "window areas," as Keel calls them. For reasons we have detailed, the standing ghost light phenomenon may well be the base indicator for identifying these locations. These places are of ecological importance for more than just preserving the environment or the genetic pool; they also play a crucial importance in preserving humanity's connection with its inherent psychic nature, with the consciousness factor in the triunal nature of reality; they are potentially our link to that within us that lies beyond the restrictions of space and time as we presently understand them.

Moreover, from what we have seen, the wild man creatures seem to be drawn to these places, the preservation of which may be critical to their survival. Depending on which model or models of explanation turn out to be accurate in describing these creatures, they could either be our most precious endangered species, or the remnant of an ancient culture that might enable us to learn about our origins and our potential as a species. This could well be the anthropological or zoological discovery of the century. If we can earn the trust of these magical beings, be they man or beast, the consequences of establishing contact with them are mind boggling.

If the energy in a space can have a psychic influence on us, then the reverse is also true. Human activities can influence the psychic energy of a given space. For this reason, the locations we seek are mainly in the wild places. Modern cities are built without regard to the subtle environmental influences of the kinds of ambient energy fields we have discussed. The flow and rhythm of the natural energies in the earth that pertain to our psychic nature may be disrupted, diluted, and dissipated by such ordinary things as the random way in which we build our roads and cities and the effects of the ever increasing electromagnetic grid we have erected. Our psychological and physical well being may be affected as well. The increase in maladies such as stress and other nervous disorders may well result from these same factors. This may produce a shallowing or scattering of consciousness, which can be reflected in our values and the way we live our lives. With this, much of our feelings of conscious psychic connectedness with one another, with the community, with the earth, and with the cosmos are lost.

One of the devastating effects of basing a culture on the materialistic worldview is its tendency to dehumanize us and reduce us to mere economic and political units. It cheapens life, making human beings expendable and condemning us to lives of largely meaningless routine. As a result, there is little cultural connective tissue, little basis for a common humanity, and little sense of a common purpose.

There is a great deal of evidence that many ancient civilizations not only understood these points, but based their entire cultures on the knowledge and utilization of the energies of the window areas. They devoted much of their science to predicting when and where the cyclic energies would be active. As Keel, Devereux, and other researchers have pointed out, they considered these places to be sacred, because in them one gained access to the spirit world, the land of the ancestors. Rather than seeing life in essentially meaningless materialistic terms, such cultures considered life to be the journey of the spirit (what I have referred to here as the inherent psychic nature) through the world of space and time to return to the spirit world. The ancestors were revered because they were those who had already completed the passage. They had made the transition from the temporal to the eternal, and had returned to the primordial reality.

Particularly among the earliest Chinese, Native Americans, and Celtic cultures of Western Europe and Great Britain, such locations eventually developed more complex societies centered around temples that honored the places of traffic with the spirit world. All of these cultures shared the central value of their common shamanic origins, which had the same fundamental purpose of aiding the soul in its passage to the spirit world and in soliciting the assistance of the ancestors by keeping the connection with the spirit world open.

This purpose was also reflected in the lay-out of their cities, which were built to be in harmonious balance with the forces of the universe, as well as to represent their view of the cosmic order. Keel notes that such peoples "located their temples, mounds and pyramids in the dead center of magnetic anomalies. And they laid out long, arrow straight tracks between these magnetic points." They believed that this connected the centers of spiritual authority and facilitated the flow of energy throughout the land, stimulating the fertility of the soil and the cycles of weather, assuring an abundant harvest, and generally keeping the world in balance with cosmic forces to the benefit of the people's worldly and spiritual well being.

Coincidentally, Bragg Road, which as we have noted is also arrow straight, may itself be an inadvertent ley line that by accident connected two areas with high magnetic energy.

The locating and building of these tracks or straight lines, which frequently were major feats of engineering, were not arbitrary. They were based on a specific understanding of what is called sacred geometry. This ancient idea, which dates back at least to the days of Pythagoras and Plato, is currently interpreted as a planetary grid of energy, meridians or lines of force, that constitute the essence of the structure of the earth. The ley lines might have been built in part to emulate on a more local basis what the ancients knew about the function of trans-global lines of energy.

In the ghost lights chapter I noted that there are standing recurrent ghost light locations around the world along a line at about 30 degrees north latitude. It may be no coincidence that the Great Pyramid lies at that same latitude. It could be one of the vestiges of the technology of an even more ancient civilization that understood and utilized similar concepts, and that latitude may correspond to one of the global meridians. It would probably be a good place to start to test the many current models of planetary grids for accuracy.

Common to all these cultures was the idea that the harmony of the individual with the society, the society with the earth, and the earth with the cosmos was possible because one is a reflection of the other in descending order from the cosmos to the individual. This being the case, if there are planetary meridians of energy, one would expect there to be corresponding meridians in the human body. The ancient Chinese medical art of acupuncture, which has enjoyed increasing acceptance in the West in the past few years, is based on a similar concept. It would be worthwhile to do a comparative study between the planetary grid models and the acupuncture meridians to see if there are any specific correspondences.

In the philosophy of traditional Chinese medicine, disease is seen as resulting from imbalances and blockages in the natural flow of energy, or chi, along these meridian lines. Disease can be cured or alleviated by restoring the natural flow of chi by a process of stimulating points along the lines or where they intersect. Again, it would be worthy of study to see if there are any possible correspondences with what might be called acupuncture points of the earth. I'll venture to say that at least some of those points will also correspond with the ghost light locations.

This view of the source of illness is common among many other cultures, including one Indian tribe of the Andes of which Gersi writes, "If people do something wrong or in some other way upset the balance in their lives, it throws their energies and inner cosmic harmony out of balance; consequently sickness, and sometimes storms and other natural disasters follow. A whole village or even a region may suffer."

They also believe, however, that the energies of a whole village or an entire region may be restored to balance. They do this through meetings of sorcerers who come from all over the Andes and gather in one village. For three days they perform the necessary ritual to ensure the restoring of balance and the survival of their villages. From this perspective, the ills that beset the modern age may be regarded as diseases of imbalance. Optimistically, I'd like to think that the same principles of restoring balance can be applied on a global scale.

In a worldview in which consciousness is equal to mass and energy, there is the possibility of a science and technology that incorporates what my friend Bill calls a deep symbiosis between our inner psychic selves and the physical environment. Despite all this talk of ancient cultures and peoples of tradition, this view does not advocate throwing out modern technology; but suggests that the element of consciousness be added to mass and energy in our technology. It is difficult to predict what that will look like.

Just over a hundred years ago, electricity itself was little more than a curiosity among philosophers and academicians. It was theoretically the source of immense energy, perhaps, but putting it to use in the real world was impractical. The development of such things as radio, television, radar, and the recent developments in computer and sophisticated communications technology, which we now take for granted, would have been incomprehensible.

We may be poised on the edge of a similar breakthrough. Current attempts to create artificial intelligence may be precursors of a time when geometrodyanmic energy inherent in the structure of space, which can supposedly be tapped by psychic means, will be employed in technology. This could give birth to an entirely new generation of high technology that is integrated with the alchemical principles suggested by Laffoley. The result could be psychotronic devices, what he calls "electric voodoo dolls," that would not deplete and cause imbalance within the environment, but would actually contribute to restoring the natural state of balance.

It may have taken our ancestors thousand of years to accumulate the knowledge of the cycles of periodicity involved with the flow of the cosmic magnetic energies and to assimilate it within their cultures. Much of the information that is needed to regain this knowledge is not given to us by the current culture. The quantity of information necessary for the development of a working multi-dimensional model of a planetary grid, which would enable us to predict the times and places of electromagnetic spikes, would therefore require grass roots participation and an information exchange on a massive scale. With the development of computer internet technology, this is entirely within reach, and it is achievable on a planetary level. Before this data will make much sense, though, and before deep patterns of significance can be discerned, we may be required to look at ourselves, at each other, and at the world from a different perspective.

In summary, I think we should listen to what the elders of the traditional peoples of the world have been trying to tell us. An out-of-balance humanity further increases the imbalance of the world. We should strive to reawaken our psychic nature and reclaim the rightful heritage of all the tribes of the earth. We should resume our proper environmental role, the deep and sacred purpose of all people who are fully human, which, as the Hopi would say, is simply to keep the world in balance.

Acknowledgments

This book could not have become a reality without the support, encouragement and enthusiastic participation of my good friends, Bill and Brenda Fleming of Llano, Texas. Through the years Bill has been much involved in the field research, not only in the Big Thicket, but also in the wilds of West Texas and Mexico. Much of the style and content of this book has evolved from many long and earnest conversations among the three of us, sometimes as we were actually in the wild places attempting to get pictures or gather data. They also have very graciously made their place in Legion Valley available to me as a retreat to do much of the work on the book. Brenda reduced production time by dragging me kicking and screaming out of my technophobia into the internet age, and has provided invaluable technical support in teaching me the proper use of a PC. No amount of thanks I can give these two would be adequate.

Another longtime friend, Jeanie Turk of Pinewood, was among the first to encourage me to write this book. She backed up her verbal support by providing office space and a computer to begin the initial phases of the writing. It was also her idea to tape record interviews at the Saratoga Spook House. Along with my old editor, Buddy Moore, and Jeanie Moore of Kountze, and my late dear friend, Steve Doukas of Pinewood, Jeanie also organized a fund-raising dinner that allowed Bill and me to present a paper at the Spirit of Place symposium at Cal State Fullerton.

A special thanks is also due to my sister, Reneé Leger Schwab, to my cousin, Judy Poss King, and to Aunt Fern Counce for making sure that I always have a warm welcome and a place to stay in Sour Lake, as well as plenty of my favorite red beans and rice and hot water cornbread to sustain me. Reneé has also helped with the photography and in coordinating publicity in the Beaumont area, and both she and Judy have helped by offering their suggestions after reading parts of the manuscript.

Jake and Sherry Boaz of Lumberton have also made me welcome in their home many times and have provided helpful criticisms and suggestions after listening to my readings of the narrative. Jake has also been involved in much of the field research, and son Benjamin has joined us on some of our recent trips. Sherry gave up on that after the deer flies practically ate her alive on her one outing with us, but she has frequently made sure we had hot bowls of file' gumbo awaiting us when we returned from the woods.

Stan Shaw and Farrell Brenner of Austin are other old compadres who have made substantial contributions to the substance of this book, both from participating in the field research and through an on-going exchange of ideas for decades. Chip Yantis, also of Austin, participated in one of our most significant expeditions to the Thicket. Betty Shaw made an important contribution by doing much of the editing of the first drafts of the manuscript.

Thanks are also due to Alice Brenner, Raymond Gerson and Trevor McCarthy of Austin,and to Tom and Sharon Dillman and Dragos of Houston for being supportive and helping me develop publishing and marketing strategies.

Cousins, John Poss of Dallas and Donna Riggs Arriola of Edinburgh, Texas, have been my chief guinea pigs and critics-as-test-subjects; they have read all or parts of the manuscript and have offered constructive criticisms. Others who have helped in this regard include Jacob Riggs, Jordan Riggs, Ginger Hunkin, Tyler Hunkin, Brenda Parker, Dimitra Doukas, Linda Crannell, Gayl Hubatch, Patricia Hubbard, Lewis Bullard, Simon Rodriguez, Mary Helen Rodriguez, and my very special friend, La Luz Gerald, who from her sweet heart speaks with the voice of the Ancestors.

John A. Keel of New York, the dean of paranormal investigative writers, besides being an example to me and to anyone who would write on such topics, is to be greatly thanked for referring me to Sandra Martin and Patrick Huyghe of Paraview Press, New York. And many thanks to them for editing and publishing the book. Thanks also to my niece, Ginnie Griffin LeBlanc, who always believed her Uncle Rob would actually finish this book.

Carl and Deloria Williams of Fred, Texas, are to be thanked for finding and returning my briefcase, which contained a word processor and many invaluable and irreplaceable notes, after I had lost it one weekend in Lumberton. Losing this material would have been a major stumbling block in finishing the book. The fact that they not only returned it, but that I received a phone call from them before I was even able to get a notice posted in the newspaper, attests to the decency and honesty that's typical of folks who dwell in the Thicket.

To the citizens of Hardin County and Southeast Texas who attended or made financial contributions to the aforementioned fund-raising dinner at Pinewood, especially to that unnamed dear lady who said to me, "Honey, I'm not sure what you're talking about, but I'm just glad somebody's doing something," and to the many friends, family members and neighbors who have told me their tales; I am much obliged.

May this book do justice to your wonderful stories.

Bibliography

Abernethy, Frances, ed., *Tales from the Big Thicket*, Austin and London: University of Texas Press, 1966.

Bergier, Jacques, *Secret Doors of the Earth*, Chicago: Henry Regnery Company, 1975.

Bord, Janet and Colin, *Alien Animals*: *A worldwide investigation*, revised edition, London: Panther Books, Granada Publishing Ltd, 1985.

Carmody, Kevin, "Strange blackout draws different theories," *The Beaumont Enterprise*, Beaumont, Texas, May 3, 1985.

Clarke, David W. and Oldroyd, G., "Spooklights: A British Survey," *Phenomenon: Forty Years of Flying Saucers*, edited by John Spencer and Hilary Evans, New York: Avon Books, 1988.

Coates, Leroy, "Bigfoot Roams the Woods Near Columbia," *True Stories from the Louisiana Bayou People*, Book II, edited by John W. Bergeron, ,Abbeville, Louisiana: Century Publishing, 1985.

Coleman, Loren, *Mysterious America*, London and Boston: Faber and Faber, 1983.

Coleman, Loren, *Curious Encounters: Phantom Trains, Spooky Spots, and Other Mysterious Wonders*, London and Boston: Faber and Faber, 1985.

Concianne, Sidney, "Roogaroos on the Bayous Near Dulac," *True Stories from the Louisiana Bayou People*, Book II, edited by John W. Bergeron, ,Abbeville, Louisiana: Century Publishing, 1985.

Corliss, William R., *Handbook of Unusual Natural Phenomena: Eyewitness Accounts of Nature's Great Mysteries*, New York: Arlington House, 1986.

Dash, Mike, *Borderlands: The Ultimate Exploration of the Unknown*, New York: Dell Publishing, 2000.

Devereux, Paul, with David Clarke, Andy Roberts and Paul McCartney, *Earth Lights Revelation: UFOs and Mystery Lightform Phenomena: The Earth's Secret Energy Force*, London: Blandford Press, 1989.

Devereux, Paul, *Shamanism and the Mystery Lines: Ley Lines, Spirit Paths, Shape-Shifting & Out-of-body Travel*, St. Paul, Minnesota: Llewellyn Publications, 1993.

Devereux, Paul and McCartney, Paul, "Earthlights," *Phenomenon: Forty Years of Flying Saucers*, edited by John Spencer and Hilary Evans, New York: Avon Books, 1988.

Gersi, Douchan, *Faces in the Smoke: An Eyewitness Experience of Voodoo, Shamanism, Psychic Healing, and Other Amazing Human Powers*, Los Angeles: J. P. Tarcher; New York. 1991.

Green, John, *Sasquatch: The Apes Among Us*, Seattle: Hancock House, 1978.

Gunter, Pete, photography by Roy Hamric, *The Big Thicket: a challenge for conservation*, Austin and New York: Jenkins Publishing Company 1971.

Hamric, Roy, ed., *Archer Fullingim: A Country Editor's View of Life*, Austin: Heidelberg Publishers, 1975.

Hensley, Dempsie, *The Big Thicket Story*, Waco, Texas: Texan Press, 1967.

Heselton, Philip, *The Elements of Earth Mysteries*, Rockport, Massachusetts: Element, Inc., 1991.

Holiday, F.W., *The Goblin Universe*, St. Paul, Minnesota: Llewellyn Publications, 1986.

Hunter, Don, with Rene' Dahinden, *Sasquatch*, Toronto: McClelland and Stewart, Ltd., 1973.

Jefferson, John, "Tales of the Big Thicket: Wild men, carnivorous plants, mysterious lights and strange creatures are part of Big Thicket lore," *Texas Parks & Wildlife: The Outdoor Magazine of Texas*, October, 2000.

Johnston, Maxine, ed., *Big Thicket Explorer*, Saratoga, Texas: Big Thicket Museum, 1972.

Keel, John A., *The Eighth Tower*, New York: Saturday Review Press, 1975

Keel, John A., *Our Haunted Planet*, Greenwich, Connecticut: Fawcett Publications, Inc., 1971.

Keel, John A., *The Mothman Prophecies*, Avondale Estates, Georgia: IlluminNet Press, 1991.

Keel, John A., *The Complete Guide to Mysterious Beings*, New York: Doubleday, 1994.

Kilman, Ed, *Cannibal Coast*, San Antonio, Texas: The Naylor Company, 1959

Laffoley, Paul, comments from a filmed interview presented at Architectonic thought forms: a survey of the art of Paul Laffoley, 1968-1999, Austin, Texas: Austin Museum of Art, 1999

Lapseritis, Jack, *The Psychic Sasquatch*, Mill Spring, NC: Wild Flower Press, 1998.

Loughmiller, Campbell and Lynn, editors, *Big Thicket Legacy*, Austin and London: University of Texas Press, 1977.

Martin, Graham Dunstan, *Shadows in the Cave: Mapping the Conscious Universe*, London: Arkana, 1990.

Michell, John, *The View Over Atlantis*, New York: Ballantine Books, 1969.

Moser, Don, photographs by Blair Pittman, "Big Thicket of Texas," *National Geographic*, October, 1974.

Persinger, M.A., and Lafreniere, Gyslaine, *Space-Time Transients and Unusual Events*, Nelson Hall, 1977.

Playfair, Guy L. and Hill, Scott, *The Cycles of Heaven: Cosmic Forces and What They Are Doing To You,* New York: St. Martin's Press, 1978.

Reneaux, J.J., *Cajun Folktales,* Little Rock, Arkansas: August House, 1982.

Rigaud, Milo, *Secrets of Voodoo*, New York: Arco Publishing, 1969.

Riggs, Rob, "It Seemed Like a Huge Hairy Ape-like Creature, said a Fink," *Kountze News*, Kountze, Texas, July 19, 1979.

Riggs, Rob, "A Special Report: Ghost Lights," *Metropolitan Beaumont Magazine*, Beaumont, Texas, Vol. 14, No. 3, May/June 1989.

Robinson, Ray, *Cajun Tales of the Louisiana Bayous*, Gray, Louisiana: Cypress Publishers, 1984.

Slate, B. Ann, and Berry, Alan, *Bigfoot*, New York: Bantam, 1976.

Spence, Lewis, *The Magic and Mysteries of Mexico: The Arcane Secrets and Occult Lore Of the Ancient Mexicans and Mayans*, North Hollywood, California: Newcastle Publishing, 1994.

Stacy, Dennis, "Transcending Science," *Omni*, December 1988.

Stewart, Richard and Turner, Allan, *Transparent Tales: An Attic Full of Texas Ghosts*, Lufkin, Texas: Best of East Texas Publishers, 1998.

Swan, James A., *In Search of the Spirit of Place*, Mill Valley, California: The Institute for the Study of Natural Systems, 1988.

Troutman, Fred and Faciane, Roxanne and J., "Les Feu Foulais," *True Stories from the Louisiana Bayou People*, Book II, edited by John W. Bergeron, ,Abbeville, Louisiana: Century Publishing, 1985.

Valle, Jacques and Janine, *Challenge to Science: The UFO Enigma*, New York: Ballantine Books, 1974.

Waters, Frank, *The Book of the Hopi*, New York: Penguin Books, 1963.

Wilson, Robert Anton, *The New Inquisition*, Scottsdale, Arizona: New Falcon Publications, 1991.

Printed in the United States
3206